THE UNMAKING OF A PART-TIME CHRISTIAN

THE UNMAKING
OF A PART-TIME CHRISTIAN

DEREK MAUL

UPPER
ROOM BOOKS®
NASHVILLE

Cover design: Left Coast Design/Bruce DeRoos/www.lcoast.com
Cover image Steven Puetzer, Photonica
Interior design: PerfecType/Nashville, TN
First printing: 2009

LIBRARY OF CONGRESS CATALOGING-IN-PUBLICATION DATA
Maul, Derek.
    The unmaking of a part-time Christian / Derek Maul.
        p. cm.
ISBN 978-0-8358-9992-5
1. Christian life. I. Title.
BV 4501.3.M289   2009
248.4—dc22   2009022459

To Rebekah, the most genuine pilgrim I know.

To my fellow pilgrims; kindred hearts on this well-worn path.

And to all those who hover in the margins—
believe me when I tell you this is

a journey you will not regret.

Contents

Acknowledgments

Robin Pippin, my editor at Upper Room Books, is generous in her encouragement; project manager Jeannie Crawford-Lee is patient and gracious; Janice Neely puts her heart and soul into author support; Mary Lou Redding exudes belief; Joanna Bradley, Rita Collett, and the other office staff never fail; Jill Ridenour markets her heart out; Jeanette Pinkston is always there; Denise Duke keeps things on the up and up. Thank you all for believing for a third time.

I have a great family; no project of this magnitude can be accomplished without support. They have always given personal faith an amazing context. Special thanks to my children, Andrew and Naomi, and son-in-law, Craig; to the resident maven of literature, Myrt; to my brother, Geoff; to Rebekah's siblings, Roy, Rachel, Joe, and Jesse; and to their spouses: Lynda, Tom, Cheryl, and Heather.

And to fellow travelers who have shared wisdom and perspective from their own journey as pilgrims in progress: thanks so much David Childs, Kirk Griffith, Jesse Alexander, Tim Black, Lee McInnis.

Lastly, a special (and possibly made-up) word to Rebekah: *Carpe Liber*—Seize the book!

Live As If
You Mean It

I press on toward the goal for the prize of the heavenly call of God in Christ Jesus.—Philippians 3:14

I love the advice *Live as if you mean it.* The idea pretty much sums up the intention behind this introduction as well as the value that guides the entire book. This life is far too important not to embrace it with absolutely every ounce of enthusiasm we can muster. The impetus initiated when God sent Jesus to be the emissary of life is so much more than I can respond to as a part-time Christian.

Recently three family milestones have caused me to think about time, how easily the present melts into history, and how significant each today is in the ordering of our lives.

First, our son, Andrew, turned twenty-six. That's not such a big deal until you realize that his dad is fifty-two. Not even my limited facility with mathematics can overlook the fact that Andrew is catching up fast. Just twenty-five years ago I was twenty-seven times his age; now the multiple is only two.

Then my brother's daughter, Hannah, entered her thirties. I've got to tell you: that's really old for a niece!

Later in the month my dad—David Maul—celebrated the eightieth anniversary of his birth: July 27, 1928. It seems like only yesterday that I stood watching my dad bury his dad, then hold Andrew, his son's first child—so tenderly—the rest of the afternoon.

"Man is like a breath," the Bible says; "his days are like a fleeting shadow" (Ps. 144:4, NIV). Maybe so, but look how the psalm writer sets up his comment about the concise passage of our days: "O LORD, what is man, that You take knowledge of him? Or the son of man, that You think of him?" (Ps. 144:3, NASB). The answer, of course, is that God found creation expressed in the image of God—men and women both—worthwhile enough to send Jesus.

Time may be like a passing shadow, but time also represents a rock-solid opportunity. We have been favored in this particular season to be present and active in a broken world that stands in desperate need of redemption. Fifty-two years? Twenty-six? Eighty? Thirty? Fourteen months? The numbers are immaterial in relation to the potential.

Bottom line is this: we don't have the luxury of surplus time to waste this gift of life on half measures. God did not provide such an opportunity for life-giving salvation in order to watch men and women opt out of all that redemption makes possible.

So why live as if we mean it? Because God most certainly means it.

Whatever age we happen to be, however fleeting our time, wherever and whenever we find ourselves in the context of this amazing opportunity to live: that is exactly where God means for us to flourish—because the way we take hold of this life means everything. That's why we were created; that's why I am so motivated to see people rehabilitate their journey; that's why I love this adventure so very much.

"Live already!" Jesus proclaims, "because that's why I came."

Full circle

Our walk with Christ is best experienced as an ongoing journey. Fact is, it's difficult to play the cultural role of "part-time Christian" if we see our lives of faith as a deliberate pathway with a meaningful destination. Following Jesus is a day-to-day process, much more about the expedition phase than the final arriving, although the two are bound together; and I can't help but look forward to the shape God's promises will take regarding eternal life, peace everlasting, and the joy of unbroken relationship with my Creator.

I remain convinced that in the here and now our life as Christ followers primarily concerns capturing and engaging the rich meaning and the lavish possibilities of abundant life before death. God's kingdom is already available, and our opportunity is to live this kingdom life, and to live as if we really do mean it.

In a sense, pilgrimage is an experience designed to take humankind full circle. *Because, if this pathway is to lead us any place at all, then that place is the garden.*

> They heard the sound of the Lord God walking in the garden at the time of the evening breeze, and the man and his wife hid themselves from the presence of the Lord God among the trees of the garden. But the Lord God called to the man, and said to him, 'Where are you?' He said, "I heard the sound of you in the garden, and I was afraid, because I was naked; and I hid myself."—Genesis 3:8-10

I'll be the first to acknowledge it is difficult to grasp the fact that God actually kept company with the likes of you and me in the garden, in the cool of the evening. Nonetheless, I want us to consider the truth of this narrative and to reflect on the limitless potentiality of our pilgrim path. We were created for relationship with God and for all the implications such relationship calls forth. I'd like for us to think about how we might intentionally step back—or more properly step forward—into that kind of intimate space.

Abide in me

When Jesus invited us, his disciples, to live abundant life as blessed children of God, the invitation was not future, otherworldly, or ethereal so much as it was—is—a concrete statement of present and continuous possibility.

> Abide in me as I abide in you. Just as the branch cannot bear fruit by itself unless it abides in the vine, neither can you unless you abide in me. I am the vine, you are the branches. Those who abide in me and I in them bear much fruit, because apart from me you can do nothing.—John 15:4-5

The purpose of this book is to engage one another in conversation about what it means to move from the periphery of belief into a deliberate pilgrim path that means something consequential in the here and now. No more part-time Christians. No more clocking in and out of this life. Living in the kingdom must challenge our perspective.

Jesus came so that each one of us might once again claim the honor and the glory of friendship with God. This is a magnificent truth. It's a truth that is sometimes difficult to grasp, and sometimes leads to accusations that I view the world through rose-tinted glasses. "Why do you always have to be so darned positive?" an acquaintance once complained. Only he didn't say "darned." I'll admit it: I really am genuinely cheery; only it's not Pollyanna—it's real, hopeful, and at once rooted in certainty. I think it's because I see clearly now, and for me clarity always leads to hope.

"Well, you're in the wrong profession if you want to be upbeat," one newspaper reader complained. "Other columnists tell it like it is."

Well, that's OK, I guess. But only if you believe that *true* is always interchangeable with *cynical* and that life remains at best a bitter disappointment. Then whining about unfairness, injustice, and disillusionment makes sense, and the diatribe will always ring distressingly true.

But here's the thing. I'm in the business of truth, and people who define their interaction with the world exclusively in terms of skepticism and suspicion are missing it, and they're missing it by a mile. I don't need to make stuff up because, as Dustin Hoffman (Captain Hook) said in the Peter Pan movie *Hook*, "Lie? Me? Never. The truth is far too much fun."

Just the other week my adult Sunday-school class discussed the critical role truth plays in our journey as disciples. "Unless we're prepared to deal with the truth," I said, "spiritual progress is never going to be an option." We'd been talking about relationships, but the conversation applies equally well to churches, institutions, communities, and nations; in fact, the entire planet.

One participant took issue with the fundamental premise. "You can't just go blurting out the truth," she said. "What if I looked at my neighbor and said, 'Sorry to have to say this, but you're ugly! You need to know the truth about how ugly you are.'"

Point taken, but labeling someone as unattractive has absolutely nothing to do with truth. What I'm about to say needs to be copied and displayed in a prominent place: *Truth is as much revealed as it is observed.* And here's another one: *Truth is a deeper reality than the mere gathering of facts.* Even information we refer to as "self-evident fact" can turn out—often as not—to be subject to broad interpretation, or just plain wrong.

> But to all who received him, who believed in his name, he gave power to become children of God.—John 1:12

"If you say you know hope, then you've never experienced the dark night of the soul," a new friend, "John," challenged me one day.

"I have, and I'm here to say that hope is real," I replied in all honesty.

"Then you're a liar," he replied, impersonally yet with just a hint of anger.

"I'm telling you the truth," I persisted, and I shared with him a little about my journey into meaningful faith.

"Then you're a clever liar." John was adamant. "And maybe I'll grant you're an eloquent liar; but I still can't even begin to believe you."

"John," I said, reading a note of despair settling in his spirit, "there's nothing in all of creation that has the authority to separate us from the redemptive power of God's truth and the healing reach of God's love."

There were tears in his eyes. "Well, I'll have to admit you're a beautiful liar," he whispered. And then he walked away.

My friend owns the right to be called a child of God; but—instead of making his way home—he is making the sad choice to walk away.

Some people insist that there are many ways to find our way home again. But I've got to tell you, I only know one truth that cuts through the barriers of time and space, doubt and fear, sin and grief, brokenness and despair, and even the cold hand of death itself. I know that truth personally. I know peace; I know assurance; I know Jesus. I know exactly where I'm going, and I know—without a shadow of a doubt—that I am finding my way home.

This is the unmaking of a part-time Christian; and I really am making progress.

Questions for Reflection

1. How does the idea "Live as if you mean it" fit with your approach to life, or your work, or your experience as a Jesus-follower?
2. How do you experience the prospect of hearing or telling the truth? Do you feel potentially threatened or liberated?
3. Do you consider yourself a pilgrim? If you do, how are you making progress? If you would not call yourself a pilgrim, how might you characterize your life as a Christian?
4. Do you identify with the term part-time Christian? If so, what do you plan to do about it?

Let me know what you're thinking at
www.part-time-christian.blogspot.com/

Prayer

We acknowledge, Lord, that there is no way to live as if we mean it and still hold onto a part-time Christianity. And so we're going to use this opportunity, right here, to make a renewed commitment to follow Jesus—nothing held back. Because that is exactly why you came. Amen.

Signed _____

date: __/ __/ ____

Witnessed _____

One

We Can't Sit on This Gospel

Or "What happens to our spiritual lives when we simply attend church and mark time?"

> And so, brothers and sisters, I could not speak to you as spiritual people, but rather as people of the flesh, as infants in Christ. I fed you with milk, not solid food, for you were not ready for solid food. Even now you are still not ready.—1 Corinthians 3:1-2

We live in a culture of growing half measures, where doing just enough to get by defines life for too many people and in too many contexts. And often, if we're honest, we have to admit that the same deficiency describes our practice of Christian faith—how we live out our commitment to follow Jesus in the routine of every day.

But there is hope, because straightforwardness about where we need to go is the necessary first step on the road to wholeness, and Jesus is all about the truth. The Master held very little back when he shared how he felt about disciples sitting on their hands instead of actively forging ahead.

> Jesus said to him, "No one who puts a hand to the plow and looks back is fit for the kingdom of God."—Luke 9:62

> Not everyone who says to me, "Lord, Lord," will enter the kingdom of heaven, but only the one who does the will of my Father in heaven.—Matthew 7:21

> Whoever is not with me is against me, and whoever does not gather with me scatters.—Matthew 12:30

What my wife's dog taught me about discipleship

I have a confession to make: I'm not a twenty-two-year-old soccer-playing athlete anymore. But I am healthier than I've been in more than a decade, and the applications to the spiritual journey are tremendous.

When I turned fifty I was excited and motivated about so many things. I could imagine all the possibilities in store for the new decade. Across the board, details started to fall into place for our family; it was as if my life was ripe for inventive and redemptive change. But there was one obvious holdout—my body! I had allowed myself to coast through much of my forties and arrived at fifty tired, soft, and—in a word—mediocre.

I needed to make some changes, but I wasn't sure where to start. Then one day my wife, Rebekah, went out shopping. She'd been gone for a long time, never a good sign, when the phone rang.

"Derek," she exclaimed, "you'll never believe what I've got in the back of my car."

What she had was a great big galumphing labradoodle puppy. You can set an alarm clock to go off at six in the morning, but it won't make you go to the gym. However, try saying no to seventy-five pounds of excitable puppy when she puts her size-fourteen paws on the bed and sticks a wet, furry nose in your face.

Three miles of energetic walk in the morning, plus two and a half more at night; then add in a couple of shorter hikes between. And don't forget numerous daily episodes of "tug the rope," "throw the ball," and—Scout's personal favorite—"chase me around the living room as fast as you can if you ever want to see your wallet alive again." Within a couple of weeks I felt so good physically that I decided to make a few positive changes to my diet while I was at it. There's nothing like success to motivate more positive behavior.

The results are undeniable. I'm back to my wedding weight, twenty pounds to the good; my bad cholesterol is down; my good cholesterol is up; my triglycerides dropped by two-thirds; my blood pressure is great; and my resting heart rate hovers around fifty.

My point is the effectiveness of a long-term intervention that adds personal commitment to the initial desire. Let me repeat that: *a long-term intervention that adds personal commitment to the initial desire.* The spiritual lesson jumped out and slapped me hard: we can want to know God all we like, but unless we're willing to become deliberate disciples, nothing is going to change. Until I got up off my duff and actually started to walk, until I modified my daily intake of calories, it was a sure bet I would remain rooted in—and to—my carefully cultivated physical slump.

Christianity is a team sport

In the natural scheme of things I don't typically choose to be challenged, especially when there's a nice soft easy chair available. My inherent tendency toward inertia was one reason it took an endearingly obnoxious large dog to bump me out of my comfort zone and into physical fitness again.

I need that kind of encouragement in my spiritual life too; we all do. Because we live in a world that's not really user-friendly for the Christian. That's why Christianity, at its best, is a team sport. Every move forward in my faith journey has occurred in the context of Christian community. That's why I need my small group. That's why the best description of my spiritual life right now is "pilgrim in progress."

It's hard for me to follow Jesus with any integrity without the following factors in play: encouragement, moral support, account-ability, a shared sense of responsibility, brothers and sisters of like mind, and the sure knowledge that others are praying for me every day. You can't find those when you're going it alone. I like the phrasing of Hebrews 10:23-24: "Let us hold fast to the confession of our hope without wavering, for he who has promised is faith-ful. And let us consider how to provoke one another to love and good deeds."

This is no world for hesitant Christians. If we are not motivated and equipped to move from peripheral spectators to deliberate disciples—as daily followers of Jesus—then we have no hope of moving forward spiritually. That's discipleship in a nutshell—being a Jesus follower in the context of encouragement, mutual support, and provoking one another—all in the context of Christian community.

Arrested development

In October of 2006 a gunman opened fire in an Amish school-house in the community of Nickel Mines, Pennsylvania. He killed five girls and wounded five others. The world, horrified, watched in awe as the close-knit community of believers responded by demon-strating love and forgiveness. The Amish ministered to the family of the perpetrator, and they stepped well outside the "safe mode" most of us inhabit.

On October 13, 2006, *USA Today* ran a commentary I submitted on their Op-Ed pages under the title: "Privileged to witness 'real followers.'" Here are a few excerpts.

> I'd like to respectfully thank my Amish brothers and sisters for what they have achieved in rehabilitating the public face of private faith. In the aftermath of such a brutal schoolhouse massacre, the rest of the world has experienced the rare privilege of witnessing real followers of Jesus ante up authentic Christianity in the face of the worst this broken world has to offer. . . .
>
> [The Amish] responded—both in word and deed—by reintroducing the rest of us to the humble spirit of the crucified Christ and the forgiving love of their risen Lord. . . .
>
> The moment a group of people begins to act like real Christians we all gasp and say, "How amazing!" Because so few of us ever really do.

The entire column was just three hundred words, but the response was overwhelming. People from all across the United States left emotional messages. The Amish threw people a huge curve, because America is not used to seeing real pilgrims come to grips with the world. *USA Today*'s readers were moved profoundly, and they wanted to thank me for helping them understand why. Such is always the case when it comes to illustrating the difference between arrested development and genuine abundant life.

> "The thief comes only to steal and kill and destroy," Jesus said. "I came that they may have life, and have it abundantly."
> —John 10:10

Christ's message is clear-cut and compelling, but we miss it so blatantly. The thieves Jesus referenced have indeed come to steal and destroy, and they have been disturbingly successful. What the thieves have been stealing and destroying is the message, and it's largely an inside job.

Steal the message?

Spending time in the presence of Christ is always transformational. Paul puts it this way:

> When one turns to the Lord, the veil is removed. Now the Lord is the Spirit, and where the Spirit of the Lord is, there is freedom. And all of us, with unveiled faces, seeing the glory of the Lord as though reflected in a mirror, are being transformed into the same image from one degree of glory to another; for this comes from the Lord, the Spirit.—2 Corinthians 3:16-18

That's not how many Christians do business. It's as if the message has been stolen. The new—highly edited—rendition exactly reverses Paul's original idea: "Let's make Jesus look and sound like a successful middle-class American. That way we'll be more comfortable because, rather than challenge us, our values, or our priorities, our version of Jesus will buy into everything we've always wanted, and we'll feel better about all the self-focused decisions we like to make."

In place of the demanding adventure God intends, following Jesus has been manipulated into one more predictable cycle of acquisition and consumption. Instead of dealing with conflict, engaging challenge, and stepping into opportunity—all in the context of faith—spiritual development becomes a kind of arrested development, stuck fast right in the middle of the "make me comfortable or I'll go find another God" phase.

We get wedged there. We try to make God responsible for our personal comfort. We settle into our highly justified "religion of convenience." It is a faith system that goes exactly nowhere.

That's what I mean by stealing the message.

That's why I say it's an inside job.

That's why I want us to take a good look at this spiritual journey.

The truth is more challenging

> Proclaim the message; be persistent whether the time is favorable
> or unfavorable; convince, rebuke, and encourage, with the utmost
> patience in teaching."—2 Timothy 4:2

There's a war on, and this pilgrim path is currently negotiating a culture that can only be described as post-Christian. My missionary friend John serves in Poland and spends a lot of time in the former Soviet Union. "I believe it's easier for me to share the gospel in Eastern Europe than it is for you in the United States," he said. "Because of the Communist regime and several generations of spiritual darkness, a lot of what I share is completely new to the people I talk with. In America people have been exposed to Christian witness for generations, and now they're rejecting it out of hand. Your battle is a different one; you have to deal with indifference; there's a sense of 'been there, done that.' There's unprecedented hostility, and it's rooted in decades of misunderstanding."

I'd add that it's not just misunderstanding but a preconclusive not-wanting-to understand. The widespread preconceptions about the Christian message may well be misconceptions, but they are deeply rooted, and they are based on years of messages delivered by public religious voices.

John is communicating to a non-Christian culture. We live in and are witnessing to a post-Christian culture.

Newspaper column

I let my faith show when I write—I can't help myself. But so many people have negative notions about what it is or means to be a Christian that sometimes I substitute the moniker *Jesus follower* for *Christian* when I engage in conversations about faith.

Numerous reasons explain our culture's rejection of so much that strident Christian religiosity has to say; if we are not willing to engage the hard questions, then we have already shifted away from the role of vital witness and have instead become a part of the problem. And it's a serious problem.

> For the time is coming when people will not put up with sound doctrine, but having itching ears, they will accumulate for themselves teachers to suit their own desires, and will turn away from listening to the truth and wander away to myths.—2 Timothy 4:3-4

The apostle Paul encouraged his protégé Timothy because he understood how difficult this particular part of the journey can be. A lot of the opposition I sometimes run into comes from people who have been abused and deceived by confusing claims and predatory doctrines: "bad religion" that Jesus would never condone. Such messages are—with the enthusiastic help of a news media that enjoys telling hurtful stories—quite often the only take on Christ's teachings the general public ever hear.

In this post-Christian culture there's a strong sentiment that says, "You Christians have no right to say anything. We can trash your faith, reference false examples, criticize other believers, make broad generalizations based on a small sample, and pretty much throw you under the bus; but we expect you to be quiet and just take it."

But—and this is why our pilgrim path must be both deliberate and grounded in the scriptures—we can't sit on this gospel, not anymore.

God wants us to shine

I'm the quiet "find a post, lean on it, and watch everyone else" guy at any given party. I'm nowhere near comfortable putting myself forward. But God has been getting under my skin and—once again—my comfort zone is being pushed wider by the day.

It all started when I married a preacher. The quiet guy had to learn to "work the room." Sometimes I stand in reception lines and shake hands. I greet visitors. I visit people I don't know. I even kiss babies!

Then I became a public school teacher. Teaching has a way of preparing you for anything; teaching middle school even more so. Believe me, I learned in a hurry.

It's all been preparation for what God has me involved in at this particular stage of my pilgrim journey. Here's how it happened:

- I fell in love with Rebekah. Then, once I was hooked, God upped the ante and asked me to be a minister's spouse.
- I wanted to help emotionally disturbed children. So God finessed the calling and put me in front of a room full of troubled twelve-year-olds.
- I quit teaching to become a writer. And now God wants me to move out from behind my desk and carry this message all across the United States.

Recently I was invited to address a regional meeting of Presbyterian ministers and elders in St. Petersburg, Florida. Best guess there were more than three hundred learned divines in the room; I was supposed to give the forty-five-minute keynote.

"Aren't you nervous?" one vaguely encouraging participant inquired just before I took the podium. "This is a huge room, it's full of people, and they're used to nationally known speakers."

"Not in the slightest," I replied. "The last five years of my teaching career I worked in a middle school. Believe me, once you've faced a room full of twelve-year-olds, anything else pales in comparison."

So God continually pushes me out with this message; sometimes to gatherings of committed Christians but quite often into a post-Christian culture that doesn't necessarily want to know. The truth about Jesus has been buried under legalism, cultural consumerism, and "Jesus won't like you if you don't act like us." That truth has been mangled by judgment and by New Age philosophy, by a kind of religious nationalism and by social good-deed-doing, by hypocrisy and by the "you can literally take God's blessings to the bank" crowd. In short, this life-charged gospel has been lost for too many hungry people. It's been misplaced, and it's going to take more than drive-by exposure to find it. What it's going to take is pilgrimage; making our way resolutely along the pathway and clearing through the detritus. It's going to take making up our minds to follow Jesus. And it's going to take inviting others to join us along the way.

That's why God continually pushes the edges of my comfort zone, and why God intends to push at the margins of yours. That's why—by the grace of God—I am able to write difficult truth sometimes in the newspaper. That's why I get up to speak in front of groups, retreats, churches, and conferences. That's why I take this message to civic clubs, schools, and business luncheons—even when the organizers thought they were only inviting me to speak about my column. That's why I am writing this book.

And that's why I am learning to talk back when people take a swing at Jesus. It's an important element of being a pilgrim, I believe; because God—more than anything—wants us to communicate the truth about eternal love.

Questions for Reflection

1. How do you respond to the term *Jesus follower*? Would you ever choose to identify yourself this way?
2. List two or three reasons why people you know do not attend church.

3. Is there anything about the way you live that might give these people good reason to change their minds, or at least to open them just a little?
4. Ask Jesus this simple question: "Lord, is there anything I can do to more obviously mark my posture as that of a pilgrim in progress?"

How has Jesus challenged you?
Let me know at www.part-time-christian.blogspot.com/

Prayer

One foot in front of the other, one short step at a time, making progress. Help me to keep my promises, companion God, and let me know the assurance of the presence of Jesus as I follow in the Master's way. Amen.

two

God-smacked in the Cranium

Do not be conformed to this world, but be transformed by the renewing of your minds, so that you may discern what is the will of God—what is good and acceptable and perfect.—Romans 12:2

Recently I experienced what I can only call a watershed moment in my ongoing journey as a pilgrim in progress. It happened around ten minutes into my regular morning walk. I always take Scout the labradoodle for a long hike to start the day, and I had been thinking about my relationship with God pretty much since the moment my feet hit the floor on my side of the bed.

Prayer is not an unusual experience for me, and talking with my Maker while exercising the dog is not out of the ordinary; walking is one of my most consistent times for deliberate meditation. What captured my attention this particular morning was a subtle shift. Normally I have to make a conscious decision to invite God in, but this time I had started the day in God's presence without a second thought—not so much a reflex as an emerging, a welling up from a recess of my natural self that typically is anything but sympathetic to my spiritual life. I had woken up with my spiritual antennae already in place; I was already attuned to listen.

Evidently I had crossed some kind of threshold. I'm not camped out here permanently, but this morning, this new day, this signal moment in faith, marked the tentative beginning of a new kind of spiritual journey, a journey into "prayer without ceasing."

> Rejoice always, pray without ceasing, give thanks in all circumstances; for this is the will of God in Christ Jesus for you. Do not quench the Spirit.—1 Thessalonians 5:16-19

Mark it down—another milestone

Of course, like the self-evaluative, connect-the-dots pilgrim I tend to be, I wondered what lay behind this landmark event. The answer came without any effort at all. It was a Thursday morning, and I realized that the process had got underway the evening before. On Wednesdays I meet with my weekly Men's Room study group. I had shared an hour and a half with my band of brothers, or, as my friend David Dale likes to say, "The Gathering of Most Excellent Dudes."

Wednesday evening means ninety minutes of concentrated dialog, questioning, study, prayer. An hour and a half of focused spiritual journeying, deliberate examination of God's Word with fellow seekers, honest struggling with faith issues, accountability, mutual encouragement, faithfulness, and love. My small group makes for exactly the kind of discipline that reworks my internal and reflexive thought structures.

I had, in effect, been experiencing a phenomenon that my favorite spiritual writer—Paul—describes as renewal via the transformation of our minds: "Do not conform any longer to the pattern of this world, but be transformed by the renewing of your mind" (Rom. 12:2, NIV).

I need some kind of renewal every day, because spiritual life is an ongoing work in progress with me. Moment by moment I am being renewed in and through my commitment to follow Jesus, as I learn to pray without ceasing, and often through the accountability and the encouragement I experience when I meet with my brothers. Jesus put it this way, "You have already been cleansed by the word that I have spoken to you" (John 15:3).

Mark it down: another milestone. God be with each one of us as we continue to immerse ourselves in this commitment to follow.

The early morning

Very often our pilgrim journey builds on itself. And so the very next morning, the recent spiritual acuity fresh in my experience, I jumped out of bed with this sense of urgency and expectation. Scout, on the other hand, needed some persuasion to make a move from her resting place; she'd snuck out of her crate and adopted the pile of "clean" clothes on the bedroom floor, folded neatly alongside my dresser, a few days late being stowed away where they belong.

I love the light that finds me early in the morning. Usually I leave the house when it is still dark. Then, somewhere in the first mile and a half, details in the landscape begin to emerge. The grass changes from black to green; the empty dark hole where the golf course should be begins to reveal its trees and contours, and—almost immediately—the birds begin to sing.

I'm not sure if color even inhabits the trees and the flowers at night, but when the light comes, the truth about their beauty is revealed in an instant. Was the color there all along? Is it simply revealed by the morning? Or does light somehow create anew at the beginnings of each day?

That's pretty much how I feel sometimes walking home, picking up the newspaper, making coffee, standing over the sink, and watching life pour over the small rise behind our house and in through the kitchen window—long shadows from the east and the morning heavy with promise. I feel made new.

The morning is a kind of altar on which I can offer what is made possible by light. Each new day is the exact venue where, at the very heart of myself, I vote on how much Christ's radical action at Calvary means to me. However, rather than subtle or otherworldly insights uncovered by candlelight, I am learning to appreciate the incisive way early morning sunshine penetrates my soul: piercing, yet with gentle clarity. Morning does not burn with the intensity of noon but reveals exactly everything I bring—or choose not to bring—to the table.

So what do I bring to the table—the altar, this new light in the kitchen window—this new day of possibility and promise? How will my pilgrim pathway refract the truth of insistent life and bring the certainty of divine communion to my journey? Is my path any kind of a clue at all when I interact with this broken world?

I don't know. But today I do know that I am committed to the light.

Always on

Every Sunday morning I show up at church early to prepare for worship with the praise team. I play acoustic guitar in a twelve- to sixteen-piece band that includes piano, drums, woodwind, strings, and a good contingent of brass. Our sound is unique, in a typical church hybrid of what's available fashion. If you had to categorize us, we'd fall somewhere around a James-Taylor-meets-Earth-Wind-and-Fire genre of sound.

We have some great singers, all the way from high-school students to mature disciples in their late fifties, but because our director is never satisfied with the number of tenors available, he wires me for sound. A couple of weeks back I was attending to a lot of details after rehearsal and before church and forgot to turn off my remote microphone. Heading back into the sanctuary fifteen minutes later, I heard myself clearly through the main speakers. I experienced a moment of panic, and quickly ran through a checklist of the things I'd been talking about, humming, or muttering while I was running around. All was well, thankfully, but I made a strong mental note to check my on-off switch in the future.

Then the whole experience got inside my head, and I realized how we all tend to carry around a personal "on-off" switch when it comes to our relationship with God. Prayer without ceasing isn't even the vaguest of possibilities until I understand and employ the principles of commitment and faithfulness that make me an open book to God 24/7. Why should it be an issue whether I'm wired for sound? Other than the fact that privacy is important, and nobody needs to be annoyed with extra noise, there should never be a question that what I'm talking about or how I'm reacting needs to be any different if I know other people might be listening in.

My pilgrimage invites me to live as if the constant reality of Christ's presence is welcome, not a threat; a privilege rather than an intrusion; not a game of "gotcha" but a joy.

Mental rehabilitation and words of grace

"A picture is worth a thousand words." True, in a limited way, but it is words—not pictures—that turn out to be the most fundamental building blocks of our consciousness. Words set the tone for what it means for us to be spiritual beings. We use words when we want to describe what we see more than we use images to interpret the way that we think.

Words help to define the content of systems we use to guide our lives. Just as computers make choices that are preselected according to protocols resident inside an operating system, our working vocabulary functions in much the same way. These loaded preferences influence our thoughts, modify the content of our hearts, prejudice our actions, and—for good or for ill—touch the people we live with.

Not only does our functional lexicon guide our thinking, but the character of our thought life profoundly affects the way we act. Words are more powerful than many of us suspect. If our vocabulary is littered—and I use the word with care—with negativity, cynicism, bitterness, sarcasm, hateful expressions, or bigotry, then our thoughts will likewise be governed by the shape of these words.

However, if we routinely learn, understand, and use words of grace, expressions of life, phrases of encouragement, and sayings of benevolence, our thoughts and ultimately our actions are lifted up; they are going to reflect the content of our active consciousness.

Doubtless we all need some degree of mental rehabilitation. Most of us have minds that require a certain level of healing, and words of grace can accomplish such a transformational task. Prayer without ceasing isn't going to happen outside of a commitment to transformation by the renewing of our minds.

Words are important because our thinking, our cognition, our articulation, our interpretation, and our communication all rely on vocabulary. Consequently, we need a spiritually rehabilitated vocabulary to process thoughts, feelings, and spiritual ideas with—according to Paul's ideal—the mind of Christ. "Let the same mind be in you that was in Christ Jesus" (Phil. 2:5).

The average working vocabulary—regardless of native tongue—

has been variously estimated between 10,000 and 25,000 words; I wonder how many of those are words of grace? The English language includes upward of a half million words, so there are certainly enough to choose from if any of us want to enrich our selection.

An individual's core lexis, then, is critical; it affects everything, from prayer and thought and comprehension, to the formulation of concepts, expression, and speech.

"As a man thinketh," the truism goes, "so he is." (The axiom is based on Proverbs 23:7, KJV: "For as he thinketh in his heart, so is he.") Jesus picks up the concept in Matthew, and the Great Teacher is unequivocal with regard to the role words play in the hearts and character of disciples:

> Then [Jesus] called the crowd to him and said to them, "Listen and understand: it is not what goes into the mouth that defiles a person, but it is what comes out of his mouth that defiles."
> —Matthew 15:10-11

As per usual, Peter and Co. just don't get it.

> But Peter said to him, "Explain this parable to us." Then he said, "Are you also still without understanding? Do you not see that whatever goes into the mouth enters the stomach, and goes out into the sewer? But what comes out of the mouth proceeds from the heart, and this is what it defiles. For out of the heart come evil intentions, murder, adultery, fornication, theft, false witness, slander. These are what defile a person, but to eat with unwashed hands does not defile." —Matthew 15:15-20

As Christian disciples we can make an ongoing decision to fill our hearts and our minds with the powerful and healing words of God. We can cultivate a deliberate vocabulary of grace, words that possess the authority to transform us spiritually. That's the power of a radically renewed mind.

Getting the cart and the horse to switch places

As a pilgrim interested in making progress, I'd like to look at the relationship between speech and character in reverse order. I'm going to put the cart before the horse.

Is it true that we simply speak in response to what is already inside us? Does the mouth always reveal the true nature of the heart? I'm not so sure. The way I'm seeing things, the relationship can also work the other way around. We have the opportunity to continually reshape our character, our intellect, and our spiritual sensitivity by first changing our elective diet of words, thoughts, images, and beliefs. I'm switching the axiom around: rather than words merely revealing character, I believe words can be employed to create character.

A dynamic relationship exists among intention, practice, and learning. The words we use ultimately seep all the way in; they slant both our thought processes and our spiritual lives. So it must be true to say that we are—in effect—continuously remaking our inner selves in response to the vocabulary and the ideas we expose ourselves to on a daily basis.

If we watch trash on television, we engraft the substance of trash into our consciousness, and consequently our psyche. If we listen to, read, and use questionable language—or defeatist concepts—or prejudicial commentary—or a secular worldview, then we remake our essential selves according to the limitations of the chosen content.

If, by way of putting one pilgrim footstep in front of the other, we deliberately read and listen to words of life and power and hope; if we guide our conversation into matters of faith; if we balance the struggles of life with the healing balm of grace; if we expose ourselves to beauty and truth, then we will find that we are actually and effectively remaking our fundamental identity from the outside in.

Either way, the context from which we engage the world around us will be shaped by the language and the images we select. In this world there is darkness and light, good and evil, malice and benediction. We will be better equipped to make a positive difference if we are vigilant about the content we allow to trickle into the groundwater of our character.

Fact is, we would all be more powerful witnesses and more accomplished pilgrims if we simply made the conscious choice to operate—exclusively—according to a vocabulary of grace.

Questions for Reflection

1. Who is in control of the words and images that flood your mind every day? How hard would it be to make some substantial changes in your core vocabulary?

2. What routine marks the beginnings of each day in your home? How would you describe your initial trajectory into relationships or work? Would you call it reactive or proactive?

3. When did you last memorize a passage of scripture, a verse, or maybe a phrase?

4. Memorize the following verse. Set a sixty-minute alarm and say the scripture aloud at least two times during the hour. Take note of how this discipline affects your awareness as a pilgrim.

Little children, let us love, not in word or speech, but in truth and action.—1 John 3:18

Let others know how God is leading you.
Share your journey at www.part-time-christian.blogspot.com/

Prayer

It's hard to ignore my commitment to follow when your words are inside my head, Lord. Help each one of us to rebuild our thought structure with the vocabulary of grace. Amen.

three

Christianity Is a Team Sport

Then he took a cup, and after giving thanks he gave it to them, saying, "Drink from it, all of you; for this is my blood of the covenant, which is poured out for many for the forgiveness of sins."—Matthew 26:27-28

A few weeks ago I sat on the back porch with my brother Geoff, talking about childhood memories. He was trying to recall the events of one particular Sunday evening at church, back when he was around fifteen. I was helping fill in the details.

My family attended Folkestone Baptist Church when we were growing up, in the county of Kent on the southeast coast of England. The building is an imposing downtown edifice with several tiers of wide stone steps that run directly from the sidewalk up to the row of huge Corinthian pillars that dominate the façade.

Rendezvous Street runs in a wide semicircle, sweeping up the hill and around to the pedestrian shopping district in the center of town. Standing on the steps, after church, we could see the English Channel, and sometimes the cliffs of northern France. Across the busy road and just around the corner from the café opposite, the crowded storefronts of the old cobblestoned high street dropped steeply to the busy cross-channel port.

My brother and I talked about a few of the personalities, the unique bones of the old building, and the familiar atmosphere of Sunday evening worship.

Then, quite unexpectedly, it was all there. I was there; we were there. The people, the setting, the exact places where we were all sitting, the actual moment. It's funny how memory can come all at once like that, the ability to pour it all out in one generous helping.

Once upon a Sunday evening

For years as a small child, Sunday after Sunday, I watched with increasing awareness as the bread and the wine passed from hand to hand, given and received in the solemn stillness of evening prayer. I watched everything; I let God wash over me; I soaked up the familiar sounds: the gentle clink of glass; the occasional muffled cough; the scuff of leather-soled shoes on worn wooden floorboards; Mr. Tracker weaving a devotional tapestry of music on the organ; traffic passing on the street below; the occasional foghorn sounding in the English Channel; Reverend Trout's long prayers; giggles from the balcony where the teenagers huddled.

It was a great balcony: the elongated semicircle of tiered wooden seating curving a full two-thirds of the way around the church. Wooden pews, constructed with long boards positioned just so, where a heel could catch by chance and reverberate with amplified and embarrassing echoes. The balcony: historic refuge of teenagers, home of the shy, fun for the adventurous, and safe haven for the disinterested.

I felt the presence of faith and communion in the sanctuary much as a child feels the belongingness of family at Thanksgiving; hovering on the edges, listening to the stories, watching the shared intimacies of the grown-ups, knowing that this was my home and that these were people to be loved and to be trusted.

Communion seemed like the sum of everything, a kind of cumulative truth. The heartbeats of the people, the color of the hymnbooks, the solemnity of the scripture reading, the hands shaken, the hymn singing, the porcelain trays designed to catch the drips from the umbrellas at the end of each pew, the awful hats Mrs. Monk wore, the long prayers, the dull thud of heavy change dropped into the shallow wooden offering plates, and the constant and exciting possibility that the choir might one day disappear through the floorboards and into the baptismal pool below.

All these were as vital to the Communion service as the passing of the bread and the sharing of the wine. And I watched the elements pass by me through the years with growing curiosity and with deeper understanding.

I watched my parents' lips move in silent prayer as they took the representations of Christ's body and blood. I watched excitedly as my brother, Geoff, made his decision to follow Jesus. Geoff was baptized; he joined the church; and then, with tears in his eyes, he ate the bread and drank from the cup for the first time.

Eventually the experience settled into my soul, and I remember my emergent comprehension, the realization that the God I already knew and loved could be known in a deeper and more personal way. I remember understanding that I could begin a new phase of my spiritual journey via deliberate personal commitment. I owned a new consciousness that I could cross the threshold, that I could move from observer to participant, that I knew without a doubt that the God of my family and my church was willing to be my Savior and ready to be my friend.

Then, chatting on the back porch with my brother well over thirty years later, drinking tea, I remembered so clearly the particular Sunday evening that Geoff had been talking about. And the memory of it helped me understand more about the abiding nature of covenant.

At that time I must have been around thirteen years old, and—along with my best friend, Tim—I was ready to make a public confession of my faith in Jesus and join the Folkestone Baptist Church.

I remember everything. Mrs. Pout sang a solo—she really shouldn't have. The Alan family came in late—again—and they clomped all the way around the balcony to their usual spot. Ms. Deed's umbrella fell over, taking her huge handbag with it. Families sat together for the most part, but a large group of teens massed in the balcony, filling two long pews.

All around the sanctuary voices joined to sing "O happy day, that fixed my choice."

It was then that my brother, fifteen or so at the time and displaying his usual spur-of-the-moment judgment, started the young people around him clapping their hands on the final verse. In my church—circa 1970—hand clapping was absolutely not done. However, flushed by their initial success, the mob barged through the choir's vain attempt to lead an "Amen," forcing everyone to sing the chorus three more times. Reverend Trout turned beet red; so did my parents.

That night—I can visualize the scene with amazing clarity—the last light of an early summer evening shone through the stained glass. The sounds, the sights, and the experiences were comfortingly familiar. My pilgrim journey took on a new sense of purpose. And I knew that God's love and presence united us all. That is communion; that is covenant.

The prayers were spoken; the choir sang "Blest Be the Tie That

Binds"; the bread and the wine were passed. And again I watched. But this time I took the tokens of Christ's death for me and slowly, carefully, almost reluctantly, I ate and I drank.

The meaning was as clear as the memory remains today. I took Communion, and I shared the bread and the wine with Ms. Deed—who was still fumbling with her umbrella, with Mr. and Mrs. Bray—who were still fussing at one another, with my brother, Geoff, with the Reverend Trout, with my mum and dad, and with that God-love-'em dreadful choir.

I shared that service of pilgrim covenant with my wife, Rebekah, whom I did not yet know; with my grandparents, who were in another town; and with their grandparents from a bygone age.

That first occasion, my initiation into bread and wine, was a meaningless rite outside of the framework of love and fellowship and commitment that was and is the cornerstone of my ongoing faith journey. My small group of friends, the collection of people I love so deeply here in my home church today were, by extension, linked with me in Christ all those many years ago: Rebekah, David, Karin, Stan, Carolyn, Peggie, Gerard, Christine, Sandy, Ben, Lynn, JoEllen, Steve, David, Carrie, Peter, and Dawn.

I felt my own lips move in silent prayer, as I do even now. Valerie, Jennifer, Trevor, and Steve all giggled when Mr. Coffee dropped his Communion cup. The Reverend Trout prayed some more. Mrs. Whatsit poked Mr. Kent—who had fallen asleep and had forgotten to pass the tray. The sounds of the organ swelled and filled the church. And we all prayed, and we all sang, and we all felt the substance of God's reality just a little while longer.

Covenant community

It's the day before New Year's Eve, December 2007; the evening is warm, temperate, pleasant, seventy degrees—Florida in December.

The car windows are down, and my roof is wide open. I'm torn between my desire for a blast of seasonal cold air and thanking God for the balmy breeze blowing through my light shirt. It's Christmas, so I opt for gratitude.

I park outside my friends' home. David, an airline pilot, greets me at the door and invites me inside. His wife, Karin, tall and radiant, is rearranging plates in the kitchen. Several other members of our small-group Bible study mill around the dining room, swapping Christmas stories and munching appetizers. At first the conversation settles around Stan's legendary chicken wings, JoEllen's dessert, and Lynn's casserole; we laugh, we joke easily, we talk about Christmas, we share fresh stories, and we converse about faith.

Then the conversation shifts, and we begin to talk about our children, all young adults between sixteen and thirty. We share concerns about their paths as pilgrims; we remember how tentative our progress was at their ages; we laugh and we share stories; Jesus is as much a natural participant in the proceedings as Ben or David or Carolyn or Steve.

After a while it's time for coffee and the sliding back of chairs from the table. The conversational weight modulates to a deeper register; more serious matters surface, and JoEllen is just about full to overflowing with joy and tears as she itches to share details from a groundbreaking family visit over Christmas. Miles away there had been a new grandbaby, renewed commitments, some strong moves toward the possibility of faith, and a growing association with a positive community of active Christians.

And, just like that, the presence of God fills the room. We experience the richness of covenant community, communion, shared life—palpable, undeniable, and our hearts jump as if they are one.

Steve shares his joy in response to prayer and anguish and impatient waiting over many months. Lynn worries aloud regarding a medical mystery. Stan expresses deep gratitude for one whole year in a job he truly enjoys. Ben talks about hopes and dreams for his family. I talk about the joy of Christmas shared with happy children.

I had arrived with no formal agenda for our meeting that beautiful December evening. There were no prepared questions designed to steer the conversation to the things of God; there was no need for a leader or any outline of events. Instead, and from the moment we broke bread together, everything we shared around the table was expressed and received in the context of powerful, living, covenant faith.

What I'm talking about is authentic Christian community. I'm describing communion. I'm talking about living covenant—not just with friends but with my brothers and sisters. I love these wonderful people; I love them with a passion; they are my companions on the pilgrim path.

This Christian journey

Several years ago one of my dear friends lost both her husband and their only child in a horrible car accident. The family was an integral part of the community of young disciples detailed in chapter 8, "Holding the Ungraspable."

Not long after the tragedy, my friend had a conversation about church with a colleague at work. The coworker was not a believer; in fact, she was hostile to the idea of God and had no understanding about what it might mean to live as part of a vital faith community. She was trying hard to reconcile her own pain, anger, and frustration; and she felt she needed to make a statement about church and—by implication—God.

"How can you possibly go back to a place like church?" she asked, almost accusingly, is if the God she did not believe in had betrayed them both, "especially after what happened to your family?"

My friend Sandee dug deep into her well-used but overstretched

45

repertoire of grace, and she answered with a conviction founded in real experience.

"How could I possibly be anywhere else?" she said.

That's what I'm talking about. My friend was immersed in authentic Christian community. That's the power of covenant. That's the reality of communion in and because of the blood of Jesus. "For he has said, 'I will never leave you or forsake you.' So we can say with confidence, 'The Lord is my helper; I will not be afraid. What can anyone do to me?' " (Heb. 13:5-6).

Questions for Reflection

1. Consider your community of faith. How are you nurtured and challenged there? If you are not part of such a community, how might you begin to look for or build a supportive Christian group?

2. Jesus surrounded himself with a group of disciples. They prayed with him; they prayed for him; they were committed to one another. Who holds you accountable and who holds you up before God?

3. If you were to ask another Jesus follower to pray for you today, what would you share, and how would you ask your friend to pray?

4. In your experience, does prayer "work"? Define "work."

Talk back. Let other readers benefit from your comments at www.part-time-christian.blogspot.com/

Prayer

Thank you so much, God of our personal histories, for the experiences that have helped to form us into the people we are. Some of us have had difficult lives; some of us have coasted. Either way, your faithful presence has defined the experience. We are eternally grateful. Amen.

four

Judge or Redeemer?

The slave does not have a permanent place in the household; the son has a place there forever. So if the Son makes you free, you will be free indeed.—John 8:35-36

I think that what I remember most about the fall is how quiet it all was. It was as if I were a player in a video, as if someone had inadvertently touched the mute button, and suddenly all the surrounding noise had disappeared. The only sound was that of my own breathing—and maybe the wind in the trees—but I'm not sure, and then the dull hollow clunk of my friend hitting the rocks below the bridge—"thunk," like the sound a full can of soda makes when it lands on concrete.

It seemed to last forever. The cry; the sound of someone calling my friend's name; the entry into my peripheral vision of something moving rapidly—corduroy. My turning, involuntarily, to see the grotesque sight of a young man accelerating toward me through the thin mountain air. And the sound of him falling, the horrible screaming silence, the blank expressionless look. It must have lasted forever.

————

After washing out of high school in England (believe me, it's a long story), I found myself confused and aimless regarding my future. I felt somewhat like a piece of driftwood that had been left on the beach by a receding tide.

But I was sure about the fact that I was a disciple of Jesus; I knew that I wanted to follow, and I was very much aware of how little progress I was making. So I got a job in a factory, attended church faithfully, played as much soccer as I possibly could, and waited for God to flag the right opening with some kind of a large neon sign.

I really enjoyed those next few months. I was happy-go-lucky and unburdened by any sense of responsibility. But I was also unburdened by purpose; so by Christmas, living back at home and taking full advantage of my parents' legendary hospitality, I realized I might have to make my move without God providing the specific directions I thought I needed. So I decided to sign up for a three-month Bible school.

The school—housed in an old mansion—was administered by a mission organization committed to mobilizing young people to evangelize the world. The place had been grand in its time and was still surrounded by hundreds of acres of fields and farmland. It made the perfect setting for young people to show up with jeans and backpacks, enthusiastic about God, passionate about the future, and anxious to turn the world upside down for Jesus.

Right off, the experience was both intense and unsettling. I was immediately excited by the fervor, yet at the same time unnerved by an authoritarian undercurrent that ran deep.

We were each assigned to small prayer groups that met daily;

lectures were always preceded by worship; we had routine work assignments that included everything from cooking to washing dishes to gardening to cleaning bathrooms; and we participated in ongoing evangelistic initiatives. The most troubling elements were the strict organizational theocracy and the sense of purposed intrusion that made occasional forays over the important boundary between influence and control.

The first teaching sessions concentrated on the topic of "submission." Our teachers made it clear that our leaders' God-given authority should not be questioned. Additionally, a disturbingly pointed emphasis was placed on the de facto authority of men over women.

I was nineteen years old, naturally apt to cultivate a questioning disposition, and owned a tendency to avoid swallowing anything without a thorough chewing over first. But I was also raised to be respectful and so resisted the allure of open rebellion.

Fortunately, I was secure in my personal faith. I knew where I stood regarding God's unconditional love, and it turns out it's a good thing that I did, because a lot of people at the school worked very hard to convince all of us that we were dangling at the end of a very thin string, that God's condemnation was ever-present—and possibly more compelling even than God's grace.

While I did raise my eyebrows a lot, I managed to keep my mouth shut. I kept a low profile, prayed, cultivated relationships with others who shared my moderate background, and enjoyed the bucolic setting. I've always been an observer, and—let me tell you—it turns out there was no shortage of interesting things to observe.

Guilt 101

One week a new teacher arrived at the school. I remember the man well, too well. He leaned over his podium with an angry scowl, and he fairly spat his words at our small crowd—already in some measure oppressed—gathered together in the spacious parlor we used for classes.

We were a good month and a half into our course, and a kind of free-floating uneasiness lowered itself like a shadow onto our small assembly. By then we'd already been told how deeply sinful we all were, teaching laced with strong doses of the omnipresent emphasis on submission. The layers of guilt that had already been applied were beginning to stick.

But this particular teacher—a preacher from another continent—well, he took the cake. He was self-righteous, he was fearsome, he used his thick accent like a sledgehammer, and he brandished his oversized leather-bound Bible more like an offensive weapon than the word of a loving God.

"We all know that God hates sin, yes?"

We nodded toward the podium, cautiously, as the cleric carefully lay out the groundwork for his argument.

"And we already recognize that we are all wretched sinners? Again, yes?" As he warmed to his subject, his dark logic played out like the plot of a cheap crime novel.

"God, we must therefore conclude, hates the sin that defines each one of us. God will not, cannot, accept or even look upon such vile and depraved sinners. Indeed," he summed up with a flourish, "God must hate everything that we are with a passion."

No mere repeater of bad news, the teacher presented his conclusions as if they were revelations the heavenly Judge had shared personally, just before charging him with the specific privilege of damning each one of our evilhearted souls by proxy.

The harbinger of ungodly doom sported a dusty suit too large for his lanky frame; he wore white shirts, vaguely dingy, a size or so too small; and his face was always red, either from slow strangulation by collar or the strained effort of contrived emotion. He would look around the room menacingly and make eye contact with each student. His heavy jowls pushed over his neckline, beady eyes boring, flecks of white spittle forming at the corners of his pitiless mouth. He stayed for one long week, endlessly stalking the grounds when he wasn't teaching, fixing the students with an intense gaze at mealtimes, sowing self-doubt multiplied by overbearing guilt. His presence was toxic, and when his taxi rolled away, the residue of his ideas clung like a cancer that would metastasize over time.

Do you think I'm exaggerating? I wish it were true. Read the opening of this chapter again. This is the kind of predatory theology that helped to defeat the young man who launched himself off that bridge. I believe religion based on fear is contrary to the invitation to follow Jesus, and I believe such a path serves to kill faith in many vulnerable followers who are manipulated and deceived.

The young man, my new friend—I'll call him Robert—swallowed all this hate speech about God and guilt and depravity. He received it as a tragic weight that his fragile psyche was ill-equipped to process. The message was presented in a suppressive atmosphere that shoved blind submission down our throats. It was, in a sense, a perfect storm.

Easily and deeply moved, Robert prayed passionately and cried without difficulty. He was always the first to confess and not too careful regarding what he disclosed. He worried me, but I was drawn to this anxious disciple and soon became his friend.

The Grand Tour

Time came for our Bible school to take to the road for fourteen weeks on top of the classes. Our community was packed on a rickety bus, and the lessons continued in the context of a whirlwind tour of Europe plus the near Middle East. The plan was to continue our instruction in the crucible of experience where we would be provided with the opportunity to practice our mission as short-term envoys of God in a variety of cultures and settings.

We visited fifteen countries. Witness, study, and worship in England, France, Italy, Greece, Israel, Cyprus, Greece (again), Turkey, Bulgaria, Rumania, the Soviet Union, Rumania (again), Yugoslavia, Austria, Germany, Holland, Belgium.

My new friend, Robert, found enough money at the last minute. Thus his tragic story became my unwitting tutor on that important leg of my pilgrimage.

In the nineteenth and twentieth centuries the "grand tour of Europe" became a rite of passage for America's elite. Our group's signal achievement was to translate that experience into a bargain-basement budget excursion by squeezing close to forty pilgrims onto a rickety bus, camping in tents, and cooking our own food.

When I say rickety, I mean our transportation was a vintage 1950s coach with a history of uncooperative behavior. We broke down before we left England; we broke down in northern Italy; we broke down in Turkey; we broke down in Romania; we broke down in the Soviet Union; and we broke down in Yugoslavia. The truck hauling all our supplies was equally infirm. It added its own complement of complications but also provided a welcome refuge from the crowded bus when I was able to ride shotgun with the driver for the day.

One mechanical failure led to a surreal picture—a large bus being towed down the highway by a team of water buffalo. Another time—with the engine disconnected from the mounts—eight of us literally held it in place as our friends lay on their backs, worked furiously, and encouraged us to stand firm.

The best "great moment in innovation" occurred in Germany on the side of the autobahn. The truck's fuel pump went out, and we ground to a halt. So we drilled a hole in the floorboards, filled a water jug with gasoline, and ran a hose directly to the carburetor below. The new fuel tank sat squarely between my legs, and gravity did the rest.

Thornier issues

> For freedom Christ has set us free. Stand firm, therefore, and do not submit again to a yoke of slavery. . . . For in Christ Jesus neither circumcision nor uncircumcision counts for anything; the only thing that counts is faith working through love.—Galatians 5:1, 6

Each hiccup or setback to our plans, we were told, resulted from "unresolved sin" in the group. Our leader held this idea over our heads at every opportunity, increasingly treating our band of pilgrims as if we were a group of disobedient schoolchildren in need of correction.

There were forty of us, fifteen men and twenty-five women, hailing from six countries and three continents. Ages spanned from seventeen to thirty-nine, with most falling below twenty-five. Our reasons for being involved in the mission were as varied as our backgrounds, denominational roots, last names, and towns of origin. But, without exception, we were all there because we needed a sense of God's direction as we made our way along the pilgrim path.

What I learned—profoundly—was how right the apostle Paul was when he wrote, "Now the Lord is the Spirit, and where the Spirit of the Lord is, there is freedom" (2 Cor. 3:17). There was precious little liberty in our broken down bus, and I don't think there was a whole lot of the Jesus I knew evident in the way the gospel was presented.

Before long, and under pressure, the confessions started. Repeatedly discouraged from thinking for ourselves, and far from home, student after student stood up and owned to the kind of shortcomings our leader had already suggested when he fingered "unresolved sin" in the community.

I believed the reason the bus broke down was more along the lines of age, poor maintenance, and an unwillingness to spend money; but several of our number took the browbeating to heart and shared some very personal sins with the rest of the group.

Eventually, in a calculated play to manipulate, our leader accused us of rebellion. We were not serious enough, evidently, in acknowledging our depravity. He became withdrawn, defensive, and increasingly suspicious. Then one morning, when some of the women asked for a needed break three hours into a marathon travel day, he publicly humiliated their "ringleader," delayed the rest stop for another two hours, then called for a prayer vigil to deal with the "revolt against anointed leadership."

I may have been offended and perplexed, but my friend Robert lacked the background of rock-solid faith required to filter such legalism, rigidity, and ego. He swallowed every word without question, constantly beat himself up, confessed every possible sin of deed or thought, and latched on to the cancerous undercurrent of accusation that insisted on labeling him a worthless sinner, too vile even for God to possibly love.

Glorious backdrop

All these issues arose against a backdrop of travelogue wonders I will never forget.

- Sneaking into the Coliseum one night to watch a full moon rise over Rome
- Mount Vesuvius over Pompeii and the Bay of Naples
- The Parthenon; the wonders of Athens; swimming in the Mediterranean at Cape Sounion; Mount Olympus
- The emotion of my first glimpse of Jerusalem; praying at the

Wailing Wall; walking through Gethsemane; scaling the fortress at Masada; the Sea of Galilee
- Mopeds around the island of Rhodes
- The Blue Mosque; the amphitheatre at Ephesus; poppy fields at Laodicea; Ankara; the Hidden Cities at Goreme; the Dardanelles
- The Blue Danube; wheat fields in the Ukraine; Kiev's young pioneers guarding the tomb of the unknowns; the mighty Dnieper River, where Charlemagne once baptized an entire defeated army by force
- Transylvania; Belgrade; Austria, and the unexpected hospitality of generous monks
- The Black Forest; Munich; Amsterdam; the white cliffs of Dover, England

At times the incongruence between our amazing journey and the oppressive religiosity was almost unbearable, and to this day historic landmarks carry with them vivid images of my friend's decline. I can't see a picture of the Blue Mosque without visualizing Robert barge past startled guards in his black army boots to proclaim that Christians need not remove their shoes in the presence of God. It took a lot of sweet-talking and most of our spending money to persuade them not to throw him in jail as an infidel.

God's love is unconditional

Guilt? Robert knew it; it consumed him as insistent malignancy destroys the cells that give it life. But what of the rest of us—watching his pain, powerless to act, and struggling too? Day after day of close quarters, day after day of travel on a broken-down bus, day after day observing a young man's will to live sucked out by his distress; what about our guilt? I know it threatened me, and I know it destroyed many in our party beyond repair.

I remembered that the Jesus I follow never moves to suppress or stifle our individuality, never seeks to take away our capacity to think creatively, never desires to put a lid on questions that help us to grow. The Master accepted his friends and invited them to share real life with him. The disciples followed Jesus out of love, not guilt; they were encouraged, not berated; his winsome way called out loyalty, not a fear of rejection.

"Indeed, God did not send the Son into the world to condemn the world, but in order that the world might be saved through him" (John 3:17). This is the only theology with the power both to save and to heal.

But I also knew the liberating certainty of Jesus, the awesome truth that God loved me—and Robert—without condition and without reservation. The fact of it had never before been tested in such a fashion. This was my opportunity to learn.

My friend Robert became so convinced that God did not, could not, love him that by the time we left the Soviet Union he had launched a campaign to hurt himself. He made a series of attempts on his life that culminated in that mad dash across the road to leap from the bridge in Transylvania.

I don't know how far he fell—forty feet, maybe—but I do know he landed just a short distance from where I was standing. He lived. Concussion, cuts, shattered hip, but his spirit was completely broken by that point, the victim of harsh teaching, hard words, and carefully cultured guilt interacting with his increasingly evident instability.

Somehow we got Robert to Yugoslavia and its more Western-friendly borders without arousing suspicion at the crossing; then one of the men accompanied him on a flight to England. I'll never forget the last serious conversation we had; it was one of Robert's more lucid moments during the long drive out of Romania.

"Derek," he said, grabbing my arm with his bony hand. "I'm afraid. God can't love someone as vile as me. Promise you won't let me die?"

"God loves you completely, Robert," I told him; I couldn't keep the tears from filling my eyes. "That's why he sent Jesus. Do you love Jesus?"

"With all my heart," he replied. "But I'm a sinner, Derek; and I know how much God hates sin. Please don't let me die. . . ."

Just a week later, housed in the apparent safety of a psychiatric facility in the south of England, Robert found a way to end his life.

Lessons learned

I'm not so naïve as to believe that my friend's collapse had nothing do with his mental frailty. But it is worth noting that many other wayfarers on that journey soon found reasons to break away from faith. Tragically, their sad long-term disillusionment cost them a lifetime of fellowship with Jesus. The fact that so many people reject Christ after spending time with Christians has become a serious reality we cannot ignore; indeed, I have committed much of my journey to healing the image of Christ in this culture.

Maybe my mission was born that day, there under that bridge in Transylvania. There are too many wrong messages in this world concerning Jesus, and I take it personally when good people are turned away from faith by those who profess Christ yet know nothing of mercy or grace.

This pilgrim way may not be laced with ease and comfort, but it is a journey where we can be secure in the knowledge of God's unconditional love and sustaining grace. This road may be hard at times, but we can count on assurance as we follow Jesus. We have a beautiful promise that comes directly from Christ; it's a truth every believer must know by heart:

Peace I leave with you; my peace I give to you. I do not give to you as the world gives. Do not let your hearts be troubled, and do not let them be afraid.—John 14:27

Questions for Reflection

1. Think about your primary image of God. Is it more Judge, Redeemer, or something else altogether?
2. When did you learn the fundamentals of what you know about God? Reflect on the sources of your impressions of God.
3. What steps are you taking to get to know God more intimately or in more mature ways? Or is your relationship to God stagnant at the moment?
4. Do you own the assurance that God loves you without condition or restraint? Do you realize that Jesus loves you exactly as you are? Have you accepted that unconditional love? If not, what might be holding you back?

Let me know what you are thinking.
Interact at www.part-time-christian.blogspot.com/

Prayer

We hear so many conflicting messages about your nature, God, but we want to know for ourselves. Meet us where we are today, we pray, and walk beside us on this journey we are taking. We ask in the strong name of Jesus. Amen.

five

Life Is Hard:
Follow Jesus

Therefore, since we are surrounded by such a great cloud of witnesses, let us throw off everything that hinders and the sin that so easily entangles, and let us run with perseverance the race marked out for us. Let us fix our eyes on Jesus, the author and perfecter of our faith.—Hebrews 12:1-2, NIV

Yesterday evening a pounding on my front door pulled me away from my work. A young man who lives just a few blocks away was waiting on the front porch, and he wanted to talk.

I pulled up a couple of rocking chairs.

The early evening air was thick and sticky; the last rays of late May sunshine caught the underside of the clouds; we looked out through the lush vegetation and under the live oaks toward the direction of his home—and he wept.

"My wife said she's leaving me," my friend said, his voice dripping with anguish. "Almost ten years and she wants a divorce. We've got these kids; but now she says it's over. What am I going to do?"

We talked. He's a good man; he's a believer; and he tries hard. We've all been there. But sometimes things simply get away from us, and we just don't grasp the issues until it's far too late. He attends one of the big active churches in our community, and he's faithful in worship; he works hard at his career—probably too many hours—but he does it because he cares. My friend loves his family, but he acknowledges he could be more patient, more kind, and less absorbed with everything else.

In other words, my neighbor is a man who finds himself one hundred percent in the middle of real life. He's committed to following Jesus, but he's kind of stuck at the moment. If he's any kind of pilgrim, then he hasn't been making much discernible progress. He knows that he needs to move forward, and he understands that it might be a solitary trail for a season. The questions now arise: Where will this path lead him? Where is the interface between his world and the kingdom of God? Is this a journey in and to some alternate spiritual reality? Or does his path start here, sitting on my front porch, with tears in his eyes and an ache in his heart so intense that it will wake me up later that night and compel me to pray?

What does it mean to follow Jesus when everything falls apart anyway?

It's not an easy road

One of the epic adventures of my life took place the spring when I spent two months as a long-range hiker with a handful of friends on the Appalachian Trail. On one particular day, the climb had been steep, the trail difficult, and the weather uncooperative. The view from where I was perched was well worth the effort, but I have to admit I felt smug because the people I had met earlier, several miles back at the parking lot where the trail crossed the road, were not with me at my glorious lookout; in fact, I was pretty sure they weren't going to be appearing at all.

"That trail looks a little too steep for me," one man said. "Besides, the overlook here by the road is every bit as good."

Nope, that's nothing but a huge rationalization. The view from the parking lot is nowhere near as good; it's not even close. I was now a bunch of miles and thousands of feet in elevation farther along the path, and I sat balanced on the edge of an outcropping that commanded spectacular vistas in several directions. The air was pure; I could see into three states. Where I was didn't even register on the average tourist's radar.

There are views, I have discovered, reserved only for serious hikers willing to strap a heavy pack and maybe a tent on their backs. Because driving is one thing; walking is something else; day-hiking is another discipline entirely; and then there is the transcendent triumph of "through-hiking." And I, in the vernacular of the backpack, was a bona fide through-hiker on the long trail—a pilgrim of sorts—making progress unimaginable to anyone not willing to tie their shoelaces, set aside the time, pull out the Band-Aids, grit their teeth, and pay the price.

———

There's no such thing as a straight line on foot, and each new day involved several side excursions, so according to best estimates we walked well over six hundred miles of mountain trails over the course of eight weeks. Hikes ranged from a short of maybe eight miles to the day we temporarily lost a group member and I logged in more than twenty-five.

Walking is fairly simple on paper, but it turns out it's absolutely critical to have the proper equipment, engage the appropriate training, and prepare detailed logistics to cover every eventuality.

I purchased my hiking boots three months early and did my best to get ready. By the time we set off from the southern end of Virginia, my boots were broken in, familiar with my feet, well-oiled, and scuffed up pretty good. But after the first day my feet still hurt like crazy—because it's one thing to walk laps and plot strategy on a map, and something else to hop that initial gate and head up the first mountain trail.

But the adventure! I'll never forget the golf-ball-sized hail, the six inches of torrential rain that swelled the streams into rivers, or the night a black bear decided to sniff out my tent for provisions. I was, quite literally, petrified. Eventually, and after what seemed like an eternity, the huge furry beastie lumbered off into the woods.

We hiked the entire length of Virginia, climbed on into West Virginia, crossed the wedge of Maryland that cuts in just below Pennsylvania, and hiked a few more days north through the Michaux State Forest toward Harrisburg, Pennsylvania.

Along the way I met some interesting folk, a few more bears, and all sorts of fascinating critters. One day in Shenandoah I paused at an "animal proof" trash can to dispose of some garbage. When I opened the "fail safe" lid, a huge raccoon—he'd been waiting inside for who knows how long for someone to come along and let him out—ran right up my arm, over my head, and down my back before scurrying off, chattering angrily.

Several events happened along the way that offer striking parallels to the spiritual pilgrimage.

Fundamentally, so long as I was moving forward, growth was my constant companion. Most first steps are difficult; I was sore and uncomfortable long before I was accomplished and satisfied. If I'd turned back after just a few days, I would have left with irrefutable evidence that such a path was not for me.

But my initial tenacity paid off. After a week I was able to tap resources I'd previously never imagined; I developed insights after a month that would have remained elusive had I not been walking in the woods; I learned more about myself over those few short weeks than I would have processed in a year in other circumstances.

We set out the first week of May, around Mount Rogers near the border between Tennessee and North Carolina. By the time we broke our final camp in Pennsylvania—around July fourth—I was not the same person.

We pushed north at the relaxed rate of eight to twelve miles per day. Saturdays we eased off, then mostly stayed put every Sunday, walking to church if we found one near at hand. The two-month expedition could easily fill its own book.

One more story fits here. We were walking through Shenandoah National Park, maybe halfway through our adventure. On this particular day, we invited a couple camping nearby to share a meal. We fell into conversation, brewed hot chocolate, and they stayed for evening devotions. Long story short, our guests were pilgrims themselves, and they stumbled into Jesus around our fire. They were so taken by faith that they shifted plans, turned around, and hiked north with our band of disciples for the remainder of their journey.

Pilgrimage is not meant to be a path pursued in isolation. Even disciples who live in community must engage the world around them and forge some kind of relationship with others who are making progress—or not—along the way. In fact, it's the people we meet who often help define the path. Because we don't take journeys of this nature exclusively to reach remote celestial destinations—pie-in-the-sky by-and-by. More often than not, the journey itself is the destination.

Reentry

My Appalachian Trail expedition lasted a little more than two months, but reentry into the world of routine was harder than I imagined. We had lived an entirely different kind of life that—in a sense—took us out of chronological time, disconnected from many of the standard elements that define the culture we inhabit.

I could have moped around and mourned the end of my fabulous adventure; I could have been tempted to criticize the contrary values owned by people who had not shared my kind of experience; or I could have buried my journey in a private place and gone along as if I'd learned nothing at all. But that's not the way of the pilgrim. So I talked about my joy, I invited other people to get out in the wilderness with me, and I applied what I had learned to my daily walk.

I simply lived in the truth of my experience.

My pilgrim path trekked right through Appalachia and circled back to civilization with a sense of consecrated continuity. God provides seminal experiences so we can learn, so we can be changed, and so we can continue in substantive growth. Then it's our responsibility to remember. It's critical we never completely disengage from such a journey—not ever.

No theme park

We live in the real world, right here in our actual lives, and this is where God intends for us to journey. There's a difference between fantasyland and the day-to-day.

Here in the Sunshine State it's possible to immerse ourselves in as much alternate reality as we can stand. Disney World, SeaWorld, Universal Studios, Epcot, Magic Kingdom—to name a few. The intention of theme park architects—Walt Disney called them

Imagineers—is to provide experiences that draw visitors into the world we experience at the movies. Guests pay admission, lose themselves (and their money) in fantasy, and then exit the park—just like leaving a movie theater—returning to the humdrum of daily existence.

One October, when our children were twelve and fourteen, Rebekah and I stayed three days in a spacious condominium smack-dab in the middle of Orlando's extended Disney territory. The accommodations were palatial; our reservations included unrestricted access to all the parks; and we were just a few steps from a shuttle that whisked us to Magic Kingdom, Typhoon Lagoon, Epcot, Downtown Disney, and Pleasure Island.

We had just moved to Tampa after fourteen years in north Florida. Reality—leaving the only friends and church and school our children had ever known—was bearing down hard. So we drove through Mickey Mouse's front gate, opened the door, and entered into a world apart. We had, quite literally, escaped, and we enjoyed a few days of fantasyland before touching back down on planet Earth to get on with our new lives.

If we're not careful it's easy to think of the spiritual pilgrimage in a similar vein.

- We imagine cloistered monks, holed up in a kind of monastic theme park, pursuing an alternate-reality life of faith.
- We sign up for spiritual retreats and shuttle from auditorium worship to seminar classes to the outdoor chapel, then back to the bookstore to stock up on provisions before we reenter the world where we live.
- We may even regard church this way: "This is where I come to follow God." "This is a slice of the kingdom." "This is my refuge from the world." "This world is not my home; I'm just passing through."

No dividing line

It's too easy to divvy up our lives between sacred and the secular. Too many religious folk equate kingdom life with pie-in-the-sky, unrelated to daily routine, creating an unfortunate disconnect between the pilgrim way and here-and-now reality.

Sometimes the separation is deliberate; sometimes it's just the way we let things become. But—always—such a divide is unsupported in biblical teaching. Jesus made statements such as, "The kingdom of God is like this . . ." before sharing stories about regular people losing coins under their sofas, workers running into difficulty on the job, homeowners turning on lights, hosts asking people over for dinner, or parents welcoming back messed-up young adults because there's something so compelling and redemptive about unconditional love.

The pilgrim path for Paul wound its way through hardship, joy, persecution, conflict, success, prison, separation, blessed community, starvation, financial distress, meaningful relationships, and finally execution.

"If you're going to follow Jesus," my friend Gerard told me, "the journey will more likely lead to ministry to the homeless in the woods behind the auto parts store than some alternate-reality spiritual theme park. Jesus isn't leading me to valet parking, a bigger house, or promises of financial reward. Every time I follow the Lord, I find myself with people in pain who need to know God's love firsthand."

My walk with Jesus will never separate me from the reality of this broken world. Instead, the pilgrim path brings Jesus into the exact niches I occupy, the reality of good news into my day-to-day. And not only my day-to-day but also into the joys, the difficulties, the fun, the work, and all the stuff that defines life for the fellow travelers I see around me.

Jesus doesn't mask reality; Jesus *is* reality. Jesus doesn't make the struggles and challenges disappear; Jesus promises to be with us, to be in that experience alongside us, to make this adventure of living meaningful and—ultimately—redemptive.

———

Reality is exactly where my friend from down the street was that sad day he walked onto my porch. Reality is hard, it's messy, it takes us unawares, and it happens to be precisely where we live. The point of this pilgrim path is to be a disciple, a follower of Jesus, right in the middle of the routine stuff—good, bad, and ugly.

Jesus doesn't promise to make anything easy, but he does promise to be our faithful companion along the way.

Questions for Reflection

1. Recall a time when you walked or traveled a long way to enjoy a great view. Remember as many details of the experience as you can. What were your feelings when you reached the viewing point?
2. What would you prefer: an easy life or a satisfying life? Which of the two do you imagine Jesus offers?
3. How would you characterize your pilgrimage? Does "weekends and special occasions only" apply, or are you on a "day-by-day" adventure like the through-hikers on the Appalachian Trail? What changes might you consider in your pilgrimage?

Share where you are on the journey; log your comment at
www.part-time-christian.blogspot.com/

Prayer

We all struggle, Lord, and we all tend to fall by the way when the road gets hard. So help us to see your way clearly, and please be a lamp to our feet on the journey. We love you and we trust you. Amen.

Six

Check the Manufacturer's Label

As you therefore have received Christ Jesus the Lord, continue to live your lives in him, rooted and built up in him and established in the faith, just as you were taught, abounding in thanksgiving.—Colossians 2:6-7

I celebrate three birthdays. One comes along every March 26; another falls on February 15; the third I celebrate every day.

I was born into my life as a person, made in the image of my Creator, in Folkestone, England, on a cool spring morning in 1956, four weeks overdue and quite hefty for a newborn. To complicate matters, the critical events played out in my parents' bedroom and not exactly according to plan. It was quite the eventful day, I understand, involving a midwife who couldn't find the address, a husband who ignited the bedroom carpet, and more than the usual amount of trauma for everyone involved.

Another birthday party I never miss is the day I became an

American. On February 15, 1985, I stood in front of Judge Vinson in the historic Federal Courthouse in Pensacola, Florida. I made some pretty weighty promises that day. At this writing—in American years—I'm still a youthful twenty-four.

Then of course there's my birth into Christ, my constant and ongoing decision to follow Jesus. I have loved God since before I consciously believed, thanks to my parents and to a positive church experience. I can't remember a time when I didn't understand the truth of God's presence and the assurance of the everlasting arms.

Eventually I realized how important it is to respond personally to Christ's invitation to "follow me." So I made my initial public profession of faith at a Billy Graham Crusade in London, England. Later I was baptized on an Easter Sunday at Folkestone Baptist Church in the county of Kent. Any day I neglect to celebrate my new Christ-life with gratitude and joy is a missed opportunity; so I do my best to remember my new birth just as soon as I am conscious each and every morning.

There are some striking parallels between my birth into Christ and my journey as an American. Both were deliberate choices, and both have involved a pilgrimage of sorts. Don't be fooled: being American is not interchangeable with being Christian, but the process of becoming naturalized and engrafting myself into a new culture has taught me a lot about what it means to claim citizenship in another kingdom.

Citizenship versus visiting privileges

My first look at the New World was classic. The huge jetliner—a DC-10—swooped wide around Manhattan Island, and I was presented with a clear view of the Statue of Liberty.

My family had traveled to the U.S. for a wedding and a three-week vacation, so the image of Lady Liberty meant little to me that day beyond the interest of a wide-eyed tourist. It was September 14, 1975. I didn't know it at the time, but as things turned out, Florida was destined to become my home. I would never again return to England except in the capacity of short-term visitor.

Little by little America claimed me.

Three weeks turned into three months. One season merged into three, and by the time I glanced over my shoulder to look back, it was July, 1976, and I was camping outside Philadelphia for the Bicentennial celebrations, singing "God Bless America" at the top of my lungs and feeling for all the world as if I belonged.

I had experienced a remarkable first year, crisscrossed the country, logged more than three hundred hours on Greyhound buses, met some amazing people, and seen more than I could possibly take in. And so, having been thoroughly immersed in America, I hopped a plane for London, packed a few belongings, and returned to Central Florida in time for the fall semester at Stetson University (DeLand) where I had been recruited to play soccer and work toward my undergraduate degree.

A key moment in my journey

> Now the Lord is the Spirit, and where the Spirit of the Lord is, there is freedom. And all of us, with unveiled faces, seeing the glory of the Lord as though reflected in a mirror, are being transformed into the same image from one degree of glory to another; for this comes from the Lord, the Spirit.—2 Corinthians 3:17-18

The DC-10 rolled to the end of the runway at London's Gatwick Airport, paused briefly, then quickly gathered speed as we accelerated toward takeoff. Then, just before the critical moment, we lurched, slowed down rapidly, and came to a sudden halt. It felt as if the pilot had accelerated hard to run a red light at an intersection only to change his mind and slam on the brakes at the last possible moment. We pulled off onto a taxiway and circled around the perimeter of the airport. Then, with several hundred passengers still alarmed, we rolled back to our starting place. A loud voice came over the intercom.

"I'm sure you're all wondering about what just happened back there," the captain's voice sounded way too cheery. "Well, we had a little trouble with one of the engines, and I had to abort the take-off. But don't you worry," Captain Optimistic continued. "Hold on tight and I'm going to give it another try."

By the time we got off the ground, I don't believe any of the passengers were actually breathing. No one said a word, and it wasn't until we leveled out from our steep climb that my heart stopped racing.

Some people travel across town to attend college; others travel across the state. I climbed in an airplane and went to another continent. I remember looking out over the wingtip, watching the Atlantic Ocean as I made my way westward; I had this strong sense of destiny. At 540 miles per hour (I checked with the captain), I was hurtling away from the first twenty years of my life and toward America at the rate of around nine miles per minute.

The idea that no one would know anything about me was fascinating. I'd have a clean slate to write on in terms of how I lived. *I wonder who I will choose to be when I start school*, I thought.

I'd be attending college five thousand miles away from home. No one knew my background; no one had to know that I ever went to church; no one would see me somewhere questionable and feel obliged to talk to my parents. I could drop my Mr. Nice Guy persona; I could curse if I wanted to; I could read dirty magazines; I could drink too much and hang around with the kind of girls who really didn't mind if I wasn't a gentleman anymore.

It was quite a flight, believe me. But it turns out that the deck was stacked. You see, I wasn't flying alone; I wasn't starting this new life in isolation; I was a pilgrim. I was, in the words of my friend David, tethered to Christ. I was being remade—lovingly and patiently—in the image of my Lord.

No matter what I thought I might possibly do to reinvent myself, I already belonged to Jesus. Jesus was my companion, not an abstract religious concept. I found I couldn't shake the Master off; nor did I want to.

A foot in both camps

By the time I completed college, I was married to Rebekah. We loaded our small U-Haul and moved north to Atlanta for graduate school. We had very little furniture, lots of music, scores of unopened wedding gifts, countless books, and a catalog of hopes and dreams.

My heart and soul were at home with Rebekah, so the destination didn't really matter. But my citizenship was still conflicted, and that summer we traveled to England for a month, not exactly sure what land to call my home.

My path as a Jesus follower resembles my road to citizenship. For many years I was a visitor—albeit long-term—to these United States. People welcomed me with generous hearts, but I wasn't convinced that I really belonged. When I spend time at church with the people I love, experiencing inspirational worship or participating in a meaningful study, I feel comfortable, relaxed, connected, and "in the zone." But sometimes—upon walking out into the world—I can't shake the feeling that I'd merely been a sightseer, just visiting in the kingdom of God.

I'm sure we all recognize the following situations:

- Driving away from Sunday morning worship, turning on the radio, entering the flow of traffic, and becoming just one more impatient, angry motorist.

- Crawling out of bed to head reluctantly in to work without a thought for God or an ounce of thanksgiving.
- Climbing over the backseat of the minivan—while driving—to chew the heads off any available children for God knows what irritation that yanked some chain and set us off.
- Greeting our spouse at the door with a litany of complaints before spending a toxic evening without a single measure of peace.
- Wondering, halfway through a stressful day at work, what the point of it all is and why we even bother.
- Observing other people at the mall, on an airplane, or at an office party and realizing that we're just like them—that there's absolutely nothing about the way we live that says anything about faith or suggests that we're any kind of light or salt in this broken world.

So are we citizens of this world? Or are we children of the living God committed to actively enjoying and practicing our status as members of a royal household?

> For all who are led by the Spirit of God are children of God. For you did not receive a spirit of slavery to fall back into fear, but you have received a spirit of adoption. When we cry, "Abba! Father!" it is that very Spirit bearing witness with our spirit that we are children of God.—Romans 8:14-16

Decision point

Such incongruity can either frustrate or serve to pave the way for deeper spiritual life. We can live with a foot in both worlds without fully committing—or we can make the decision to follow Jesus. Being a Jesus follower involves more than visiting or "affiliate membership"; it has to become a deliberate way of being.

My journey to citizenship here in the United States reached its critical tipping point exactly that way.

When Rebekah and I were both twenty-six, our young family moved to Pensacola, Florida. We had an infant child, Andrew, and I was pursuing a degree in education. My life in America was taking on the workaday shape of family and responsibility and church and taxes and future. Yet when I traveled, my passport still read "British Subject: Citizen of the United Kingdom and Colonies."

Epiphany for me arrived in response to our next visit to England; it was the summer of 1983. We were there to attend my grandfather's funeral.

My spirit felt curiously unsettled. At first I thought it was related to the loss of my grandfather, but as the trip progressed, I realized I was actually a stranger in the land of my birth. I had to concentrate hard to drive on the left. My idiom had shifted; I didn't get the TV shows; the game of cricket on the village green appeared quaint rather than captivating. And when I walked the streets surrounding my childhood home, the familiarity drained with each step.

I started to act like a tourist. But what I really felt like was a refugee.

When we returned to the United States, our little family had to split up at immigration because I entered through the "Foreign Nationals" line. An hour or so later we were in the air again and bound for Florida.

I turned to Rebekah. "I'm not confused anymore," I said.

"What do you mean?" she asked.

"The moment our wheels touched U.S. soil I knew that I was home," I said. "Now we're back, I realize why England felt so different on this visit. It's time I filed my citizenship papers."

It wasn't a matter of expediency, of making my life in the USA simpler, or even that I'd been anxious to vote. It turns out I already was an American: I knew it in my heart. Now I was ready to take deliberate steps in order to add commitment to the equation, because making that kind of a decision is serious business.

The tipping point for Jesus

Making the decision to become a Jesus follower, years previously at Billy Graham's London crusade, was much the same as my realization that the USA was—already—my home. God was already a very real and vital part of my life. I loved God, and I knew that God loved me; yet I still felt as though I had a foot in both camps.

A section of the United States Citizenship Oath is instructive in thinking about our decision to follow Jesus. It goes like this: "I absolutely and entirely renounce and abjure all allegiance and fidelity to any foreign prince, potentate, state, or sovereignty of whom or which I have heretofore been a subject or citizen; . . . I will support and defend the Constitution and laws of the United States of America against all enemies, foreign and domestic; . . . I will bear true faith and allegiance to the same."

That's powerful stuff. I can remember the scene in the Federal courthouse like it was yesterday. The room was crowded with people. I stood. I faced the judge. I placed my hand on my heart. In just a few moments I was no longer going to be British (this is the part my mother still refuses to accept in any way, shape, or form).

I couldn't in good faith be British anymore; it's the exact reason why I don't believe in dual citizenship. "Oh, I still use my British passport," people tell me; "I'm a citizen of both nations." Well, I'm sorry, and I mean no offense, but if you took the oath (excerpted above) and still insist you're a citizen of another country, then you have to be lying to somebody.

I knew the exact same powerful truth about Jesus when I listened so intently to Billy Graham's message back when I started this journey. When I made the decision to follow my Savior, I understood that it meant I wasn't merely a visitor anymore. I don't think I'd ever understood so clearly what it means to live as a pilgrim in progress. "The kingdom of God is like this," Jesus was fond of saying, "and this, and this, and this. . . ."

Christ taught a kingdom life that is a citizenship we must take steps to claim—wherever we are, irrespective of any other membership, privileges notwithstanding. No more part-time Christian but adopted children of God.

Questions for Reflection

1. Do you consider yourself a citizen of God's kingdom, or do you perhaps still hold two passports?
2. Make a list of at least five key moments in your journey as a pilgrim in progress. Is this maybe one of those moments?
3. If you make a decision for Jesus, who are the first people you would tell? Are there people you would rather not tell? If so, why do you feel that way?

Share some details of your Jesus story with me and others.
Go to the conversational blog at
www.part-time-christian.blogspot.com/

Prayer

This pilgrim path is not an easy route to take, God, but we want to be more resolute about our intention to follow Jesus. Please encourage us along the journey, and thank you for adopting us as your full-time children. Amen.

seven

Subversive
for Jesus

If with Christ you died to the elemental spirits of the universe, why do you live as if you still belonged to the world? Why do you submit to regulations?—Colossians 2:20

My POGS crowd (parents of grads) gets together every Sunday evening. It's a small-group Bible study for those of us who used to be parents of teens (POTS). Then one day we noticed our children had moved off to college and beyond.

One topic of constant prayer concerns the influence the ambient culture impresses on young adults. Then, once we begin to think about it, we end up praying for ourselves too, because the same forces are hammering away at all of us. That's where our conversation had settled the evening we turned to the second chapter of Colossians. "If with Christ you died to the elemental spirits of the universe, why do you live as if you still belonged to the world?"

It's a good question: Why do we allow ourselves to be pushed around by the world?

As we talked, I asked my friends to come up with some words that might properly describe the posture of a pilgrim in such a scenario; how might we overcome "elemental spirits," and how might we, as Jesus followers, deal with the tendency we all slip into, to "live as if [we] still belonged to the world"?

Prayer, Bible study, accountability to other believers, a disciplined devotional life, all these ideas came out as useful suggestions. Then the Holy Spirit touched somebody—I believe it was Peggie—and she said one word, "subversive." Suddenly we knew what we all had to do.

We talked about ways we can lead Christ-directed lives of cultural subversion. How can we take the offensive, especially in terms of living in such a way that the manner in which we follow Jesus will undermine the very things that seek to destroy faith?

Can we, practically speaking, lead lives of such Christ-directed power that the culture we inhabit might literally be re-formed because we dare to follow Jesus? The answer is a most definite yes! In fact, leading such lives is our responsibility as emergent reformation pilgrims. Subversion quite possibly may be our calling.

"Set your minds on things that are above," Paul goes on to say in the next chapter of Colossians, "not on things that are on earth, for you have died, and your life is hidden with Christ in God" (Col. 3:2-3).

Wasn't the Reformation finished 500 years ago?

Many of us live out our faith as if the Protestant Reformation was a one-time incident, fixed in time and space. Things got a head of steam going in 1517, the year Martin Luther nailed his famous protest document to the church door in Wittenberg. Luther's subversive act was simply one more nudge, an act of conscience that tipped the balance of protest beyond the point of return. But, to look at much of the history of the Christian church, you'd think Luther's reformation was wrapped up, packed up, and put to rest by sometime around 1520.

Both individuals and institutions have a tendency toward spiritual inertia. But the concept of reformation—reforming, improving, renovating, reinvigorating—is by definition a present and ongoing movement. The contemporary "emergent" church movement (ditto for an emergent personal faith) reflects the same principle; "emergent" describes what is going on with much of the body of Christ in response to the insistent urging of the Spirit, as God's eternal purposes interact with an ever-changing world.

As a Presbyterian I find all of this deliciously ironical. Presbyterians are among the loudest and proudest when it comes to touting "our reformed heritage," yet so many congregations dig their heels in and resist change with a passion (we also tend to resist passion with a passion, but that's another subject!).

Of course, this inflexibility is not limited to one denomination. If your church identifies with Protestantism in any shape or variety, chances are the idea of actual transformation is often perceived as threatening—both individually and corporately: "Don't make me uncomfortable; I come to church for strokes, reassurance, familiarity, and tradition." Then there's the classic, "We're a specialized, traditionally focused worshiping community. People should either learn to appreciate our customs or find a church more suited to their taste."

Seven deadly words

When we first arrived at our church in Brandon, Florida, my wife, Rebekah, addressed the idea of reformation versus stagnation head-on. One of her first sermons dealt with what she still refers to as the seven deadly words of the church. Those seven words are "We've never done it that way before." They amount to a mantra of un-reformation, testimony to the sad reality that many churchgoers actually venerate tradition and habit more than they worship the living God.

Whether it's the "correct" hymnbook (you know, the one we grew up with) or the "only" tune for the doxology (the one we grew up with) or an insistence that the preachers wear robes—or not (like they did—or didn't—when we grew up) or disdain for guitar accompaniment (we didn't have that when I was growing up) or the arrangement of the pews (not like it was when St. So-and-So was pastor) or even something imaginative like stepping away from the pulpit to read the scripture in "storytelling" style (that's just not right)—the "We've never done it this way before" crowd always has a hard time.

Why? Because a great many people come to church not so much to seek Jesus as to find comfort in familiarity and ritual.

Seven life-giving words

In that sermon Rebekah went on to offer some alternative, "life-giving" words, a radical contrast to the other seven. The Bible is a much better basis for emergent faith than our own personal prejudices. The seven life-giving words are simple: "I can do all things through Christ" (Phil. 4:13, KJV).

The culture of "I can do all things" responds with joy and anticipation to the dynamic Christ-life. "I can do all things" is a deliberate way of being, a lifestyle activated in worship and mission as a straightforward response to the Jesus imperative that invites, always, "Leave your nets and follow me" (Matt. 4:18-22, paraphrase).

"I can do all things" offers an unhesitant yes. Yes to Jesus, yes to belief, yes to life, yes to faithfulness, yes to reformation, yes to transformation.

The unmaking of a part-time Christian

Jesus gives us the strength to loose the chains of what I have come to understand as part-time Christianity. Too many of us consistently relegate faith in Christ to part-time status.

- Church makes me feel good, but let's not get carried away.
- There's too much extremism going around. I'm not about to go down that road. God should not be intrusive.
- God is important to me; faith is pretty high up on my list.
- I like my religion carefully calibrated to avoid rocking my status quo.
- Fine, if we don't talk too much about the uncomfortable "cross" thing.
- I've got other priorities, you know. If anyone gets pushy about this God stuff, then I'm not kidding, I'm "out of here." You won't see me this side of Christmas.

Part-time misses the heartbeat of what makes following Jesus so exciting. My experience of ministry in and through the church—along with my wife, Rebekah—has been one long satisfying adventure from day one.

There's a lot of press out there that tags mainline churches as the poster children for widespread decline. Methodist, Presbyterian, Baptist, Lutheran, Episcopalian, UCC—we've all read the doom-and-gloom denominational reports, and we're well aware how difficult it has become to be effective witnesses for new life in Christ. But Rebekah and I have experienced an across-the-board constant affirmation that, as Paul proclaimed so eloquently in 2 Corinthians, "No matter how many promises God has made, they are 'Yes' in Christ" (1:20, NIV).

Not hobbled by the status quo

Maybe Rebekah and I have had an unreasonable advantage because neither one of us quite fit the basic requirements for ministry out of the box. She still jokes that she failed the physical from day one; but the question *What do you do with a female pastor?* is still difficult for some people to process. Then the question *What on earth is a preacher's husband supposed to do?* may well be more challenging still. It's been fairly easy to avoid the pitfall of mimicking the status quo, because for us there is no stereotype, no limiting set of expectations, and no pigeonhole where we're expected to roost.

When Rebekah and I first met, we were both undergraduates at Stetson University in central Florida. I had absolutely no clue as to what my future held. Rebekah, on the other hand, had felt God's call to ministry ever since she had been in elementary school. It was a certainty she put to good use. When people questioned how I'd cope with the challenge of being a "preacher's husband," I could honestly say I had no expectations, no preconceptions, and no role models to follow going in.

So we weren't hampered—*hobbled* might be a more accurate word—by narrowly defined social and professional norms. These roles—restrictive at best—have merged over many decades with the ambient way of life. The assigned parts more typically resemble a stylized Hollywood image of "Mainline North American Church" than the insistent urgings of the Spirit of God.

You'd think the gospel would be cutting edge; and, of course, it is. But I've got to say—and I'll do this as gently as possible—I'm not sure that the heart of the gospel of Jesus is in actuality being preached that much in the established church as we know it. What's being preached instead is a kind of torpid religiosity. We're entrenched in tradition and practice more than we are rooted in Christ. It's one more reason the church is having such a hard time.

My wife attended seminary in order to earn her master's degree in divinity and to prepare for ministry, but she was also obliged to fight an insistent demand that she blend in with the institutional playbook. "Conform or perish" was the rule if she wanted even the slightest chance to make it as a professional in the church.

"Conform or perish" translated into doing everything short of surgery to look, act, and sound like a man. Short hair, unisex clothing, clerical collars, harder edges, corporate ladder climbing. "Try to lower your voice," one professor chided; "you sound too much like a woman." "Your hair is distracting me," another said; "you should get a more masculine cut."

Women forged a template of cautiously muted femininity in order to stay afloat. But Rebekah said she was called to follow Jesus "without reservation," not deny who she is, compromise, or try to sneak in the backdoor.

The seminary president tried to dissuade Rebekah from marrying: "It doesn't work for married women to pastor churches," he'd told her. Later, when we were expecting our first child, she was called in once again. "I don't want you interviewing with pulpit search teams while you're pregnant," he directed. "No one will hire you, and a woman looking for work while expecting a baby will be a negative reflection on the seminary." She smiled respectfully, excused herself, and continued to follow the urgings of the God whose sense of timing has always been so much more effective than ours.

God, of course, had exactly the right church in mind, and when Trinity Presbyterian extended a call to Pensacola, we decided I would stay home for our baby's first year, then go back to school and get a teaching job when he was two. It set the tone for a shared child-raising plan that broke new ground for dads. One reason ministry has worked out so well for us over the past thirty years is our refusal to play the assigned parts.

We started out in the early 1980s, a time when few women were in ministry and even fewer serving active or growing congregations. So my joy has been the opportunity to help define the role of the minister's husband.

Listen to the spirit; follow Jesus

If there's one model both Rebekah and I have constantly fought hard to disprove, it's the idea that faith should in any way be formulaic, stereotypical, one-size-fits-all, or easy to define. God, it turns out, is much harder to pin down than that. Rather than feeling like disadvantaged victims of sexism or discrimination, it worked to our spiritual advantage to show up at Rebekah's first ministry job and find we both had to start from scratch. There were no preconceptions, no time-honored parts to play, and no predetermined expectations other than the call to follow Jesus.

That's what "emergent" really means: we simply follow Jesus. Our worship, service, illumination, spiritual growth, prayer life, our journey into Christ—all these things—emerge in response to the primary and critical priority of regarding everything else "as rubbish, in order that I may gain Christ" (Phil. 3:8).

Questions for Reflection

1. Why do you think tradition so often trumps Jesus in the religious community?
2. Be honest: sometimes wouldn't you rather be comfortable than faithful? What are some ways that following Jesus make you uncomfortable?
3. If you find it difficult to follow Jesus in your work environment, what do you do?
4. Do you have Christian friends committed to challenging you

and holding your feet to the fire of faith? If not, how could you begin to build a network of friends who hold one another accountable?

5. Think of times when you have experienced or observed faith as countercultural in our society. How have those situations or events affected the way you live out your faith?

What are you doing to infiltrate this culture with the good news?
Share your story at
www.part-time-christian.blogspot.com/

Prayer

We understand how important it is to live in this culture so we can be witnesses here. But save us from mediocrity, Jesus, and teach us how to be subversive Jesus followers in the day-to-day world. Amen.

eight

Holding the Ungraspable

And straightway the father of the child cried out, and said with tears, Lord, I believe; help thou mine unbelief.—Mark 9:24, KJV

Rebekah and I had been married three years when she completed seminary in Atlanta. That summer she was called as associate pastor and ordained as "minister of word and sacrament" at Trinity Presbyterian Church in Pensacola, Florida. We were young; we were just starting out; it was an exciting time.

We had an eight-week-old baby.

We were moving to Florida's Gulf Coast.

We purchased our first house.

Rebekah was launching her career.

It was my turn to go back to university.

We were broke; we were happy; we were full of hope.

However, even though Rebekah was on staff, and our new

church reached out as a generous and loving community, we still felt a little lonely and disconnected. Graduate school in Atlanta had been intense and focused; it was an experience we shared with around 150 other students, all moving in the same direction. We all lived on the same campus; we all talked about the same issues; we all met at the cafeteria, the library, the common areas, and the chapel. We strolled the lawns and the pathways together, playing Frisbee golf and dialoguing about family, theology, and life. Our time together had all the qualities of indisputable community.

But our new home was suburbia and sprawl, with potential friends scattered over twenty square miles. The church may have been a wonderful gathering place; but, with regular attendance mirroring the 40 percent average of most mainline congregations, we could go weeks without running into some of our peers. So, and because we didn't know any better, my wife and I created a new community within the church—and we invited everyone to come who we suspected might be in the same boat.

Within a few weeks, a core group of thirty young adults were gathering on Sunday mornings for nurture and Bible study. During the week, we drank a lot of coffee and tea in neighborhood homes. We served together in mission projects, watched movies, shared common meals, went to the beach in large groups, helped each other with home improvements, and—most importantly—we shared our faith stories and we prayed, we prayed, we prayed.

Over the years, the class grew, with as many as one hundred showing up for our Sunday morning discussions—that's huge for a traditional Presbyterian congregation. And later, as our children grew to grade-school age and then early adolescence, we supported and loved one another in the midst of the chaos. We prayed, listened endlessly, cried together, and even provided no-questions-asked "sanctuary" for one another's children when our offspring drove us crazy.

In short, we achieved a certain *koinonia* (anglicized version of the Greek term meaning "community" or "fellowship"). Much like the experience Rebekah and I enjoyed at graduate school in Atlanta, our spiritual life once again became the kind of intense, focused, shared life in Christ necessary for engaging the spiritual journey with purpose and forward progress.

Honest doubt and genuine story

I've always appreciated the value of candid dialogue. My experience, as I talk with and interview such a wide variety of people, consistently confirms the truth of the saying "The unexamined life is not worth living," a proverb the philosopher Socrates coined when addressing a jury in Athens (399 BCE).

Consequently I have always held that honestly felt and thoughtfully expressed doubt is a beneficial component of bona fide Christian faith. Faith becomes unnecessary in the face of slick orthodoxy, and I am especially nervous of people who profess to have all the answers. The trite or self-righteous dismissal of genuine questions is a debilitating turnoff for pilgrims searching for the truth about themselves and about God.

Straightforward dialogue is the way I learn best, and it's the culture we intentionally developed in the young-adult Christian community that evolved around the Kaleidoscope adult Sunday school class Rebekah and I facilitated for more than a decade in our Pensacola church.

This band of Jesus followers was so attractive that several nonbelievers started to attend—usually with their churchgoing spouse; they were, in a sense, pre-pilgrims just starting out. They showed up week after week because they valued the open discussion, liked being with people who loved them, and enjoyed the spirit of Christian community—it resonated in places that gave them hope.

Rob Bell (Mars Hill Bible Church) suggests that unbelievers are often attracted to church because the truth about God's generous love can transcend even the most strident atheism.

> What are human beings
>   that you are mindful of them,
> mortals that you care for them?
>
> Yet you have made them a little lower than God,
>   and crowned them with glory and honor.
> You have given them dominion over the works of your hands;
>   you have put all things under their feet.—Psalm 8:4-6

I think Bell is right. God's glory reaches out to people. It strikes an internal chord of genuineness, and the truth of it can work its way into the most desperate places. Responding to a loving God is the most natural thing in the world; fact is, we have to work hard to reject such a winsome invitation.

One young man, Ed, accompanied his wife to our Pensacola church. His parents were longtime members, and he knew a lot of other people who attended. In that culture, such affiliations were very much socially beneficial. He did not hide the fact, however, that he certainly was not a believer. We invited Ed into our community. His wife had jumped in immediately, and Ed would show up for most social gatherings. Then, and because he felt completely welcome, he started to come to Sunday school classes too. Little by little, encouraged by challenging lessons, stimulating conversation, a community that lived large for Jesus, and a true spirit of acceptance—plus of course the really good coffee and doughnuts—my friend not only became a Sunday morning regular but put in his two cents' worth during an increasing number of discussions.

Ed—the pilgrim—felt secure enough to ask penetrating questions and to doubt eloquently; and, because he was respected by those who did believe, he returned the courtesy even when he felt frustrated by the conclusions we would reach. The status quo remained unchanged over several years—a brilliant yet skeptical mind, unable to accept Jesus as Lord yet at the same time unable to deny the presence of God's glory among the people he loved.

Then, one quiet Sunday morning and in front of maybe sixty people, Ed sidled up to the front of the room.

"Derek, I've got something I want to say to the class," he said, a little hoarsely.

"The floor's all yours," I responded.

Ed stood off to the side a little, hands deep in his sport-coat pockets, and cleared his throat. "I just want to say this one thing."

We waited, interested to see what ground our friend would stake out this time.

"Lord, I believe," he said, in his best King James English, "help thou mine unbelief."

You could have heard a pin drop.

Believing is seeing

The skeptic says, "Seeing is believing." But the pilgrim learns that "believing is seeing." The writer of John's Gospel makes it very clear that in our spiritual lives believing is the necessary precursor to seeing anything at all.

"Jesus said to her, 'Did I not tell you that if you believed, you would see the glory of God?'" (John 11:40).

"I have come as light into the world, so that everyone who believes in me should not remain in the darkness. I do not judge anyone who hears my words and does not keep them, for I came not to judge the world, but to save the world" (John 12:46-47).

"Jesus said to him, 'Have you believed because you have seen me? Blessed are those who have not seen and yet have come to believe'" (John 20:29).

Yet we want our evidence, and we want it laid out exactly our way. Which is funny when you think about it, because the moment we prescribe what kind of criteria the Creator is obliged to meet in order to pass muster with our particular belief systems, then we have essentially put a lid on the glory of almighty God.

In the very act of demanding verification, we promote our own selves to God and in the same breath diminish God's transcendent dimensions to measurements more readily imagined by such a small deity as ourselves. Absurd, isn't it?

Jesus anticipated such problems when he reminded us that it is belief that ignites the light of truth, and then it is Christ's light that serves to illuminate the darkness. It remains one of those logical fallacies—or non sequiturs—to first wait for evidence that is small enough for us to grasp in order to believe in God, who is beyond grasping at all.

Belief that expects action

This chapter began with the move my wife and I made to her first church after graduate school. The way God confirmed the calling to Florida illustrates what God has been teaching both of us about belief.

We were expecting our first child when Rebekah initially interviewed for the associate pastor's position in Pensacola. The conversation was very positive, and so the personnel team invited both of us to spend a weekend in deeper conversation with the church.

We left Atlanta on a cold, wet March day and arrived on the Gulf Coast just a few hours later, welcomed with eighty degrees and perfect sunshine. The weekend went positively in every respect, but the clincher—for me—came when a church member took us out on his yacht for lunch, right after church. I was sold, hook, line, and sinker; no need for further review.

Rebekah, on the other hand, the person actually interviewing for the job, was more concerned with discerning God's call.

"What's up with that?" I joked. "What could be clearer than perfect sunshine, fine dining, and sailing on the Gulf of Mexico?"

"I'll tell you what," she replied, "I'm going to ask God for a sign."

This was not good news for me. What if God got it wrong and we ended up moving to a church somewhere in the Midwest in the middle of a snowstorm?

It was late in the evening, and we were driving north, from Montgomery to Atlanta, on Interstate 85.

"You know where the road crests that certain hill and, all of a sudden, the lights of the city are visible for the first time?" Rebekah said.

"Yes," I replied, cautiously. "What about it?"

"Well, I'm asking God for a blackout," she continued. "If God wants us to go to Pensacola, then the entire city of Atlanta will be off the grid."

"Wait just a second," I jumped in. "Do you know how many transformers would have to be out? How many substations? How many power plants? No way; your idea is entirely unreasonable."

She laughed, kind of like the angel Gabriel right after he delivered the "guess what?" news to Mary at the opening of the Christmas story; "For nothing will be impossible with God" (Luke 1:37).

I sweated it out for somewhere around thirty miles before we came to the high point on the Interstate my wife had in mind. I slowed down involuntarily, subconsciously delaying the end of my Gulf Coast fantasies.

The road was fairly busy, with a steady stream of cars heading in both directions, and I made my eyes squint tight against the oncoming headlights to better watch my dreams die. We crested the hill, passed the spot, and suddenly I couldn't see a thing—nada, zero, nothing, zilch, zip. We had run into a bank of fog head-on at around sixty miles per hour. We couldn't see fifty feet in front of the car, let alone the lights of Atlanta.

I'm not sure, but I'm pretty positive that in the back of my mind, certainly in the back of my heart, I heard God chuckling. "It's not about empirical proof," God seemed to say, between guffaws, "you either believe, or you don't. I want you—both of you—to learn how to trust me."

Belief is a fundamental accessory to carry with us along the pilgrim way; belief makes it possible to see more clearly. My wife and I had to make a decision based on faith, based on our knowledge of God's word for us and our experience with the personal gifts God had already given. Then, with trepidation maybe, it was up to us to walk into our future, to step into belief with our faith in God's goodness and providence intact.

In my ongoing spiritual story, the whole "belief" equation has been all over the map. But I do understand, with great clarity, that belief for the purposeful pilgrim is more a decision that an emotional response. Belief is something I have always had to step into rather than simply experience. But I can count on God's faithful response always to be there, without fail, consistently, and to buoy my intention once I begin the journey.

It's as if God thrives on my taking Jesus at his word.

Questions for Reflection

1. Are you a "seeing is believing" kind of Jesus follower, or have you discovered that "believing is seeing"? Write or share an example.

2. When have you asked God to help you with your doubts? What happened?

3. Name any belief issues you are struggling with on your journey today. Write a short prayer in the space provided.

Holding the Ungraspable

Start with the words, *Lord, I want to be honest about my doubts.*

Are you moving forward on your pilgrim path or are
you stuck? Talk about your journey at
www.part-time-christian.blogspot.com/

Prayer

*Thanks for encouraging us in our belief, Lord. We're grateful that you are
right there with us, even in the middle of our doubts. We want to commit
ourselves to your way more completely. Amen.*

nine

Reversing Columbine

> Be strong, be courageous, and keep the charge of the LORD your God, walking in his ways and keeping his statutes, his commandments, his ordinances, and his testimonies.—1 Kings 2:2-3

The large room buzzed with anticipation and comfortable friendship. Baby boomers and teens rubbed elbows easily; flash cameras recorded wide grins for posterity; parents exchanged greetings; proud graduates showed off shiny new yearbooks; a formally attired waitstaff composed of tenth- and eleventh-grade students whisked fresh hors d'oeuvres and frothy punch in and out of the gathering.

The occasion was the annual good-bye dinner for twelfth-grade students at our Brandon church in the suburbs east of Tampa. After sharing a blessing, the eager grads and their parents moved into the dining room across the hall—along with several more of us privileged to play a leadership role in the church. We sat around beautifully decorated tables, chatted with the young people, and exchanged funny stories, enjoying the evening.

Some of the youth advisers and family members had prepared a gourmet meal. The tables were served by the younger teens, who knew their turn would come soon enough. Then, one by one, as the desserts began to disappear, mothers and fathers stood up to speak about their offspring, the product of eighteen short years.

"We are enormously proud of you, Kim," Steve said. "There has been so much for you to navigate, to deal with. But here you are—rock solid and grounded in your faith."

"Chris, I remember holding you in a rocking chair," Ben wiped a moist eye, "the one your grandfather held me in, and I was thinking *Oh-my-gosh, you will never be this small again!* Here you are, and you have faced tough times and made good choices. We are both so proud."

Karen smiled wistfully; Kirk is their youngest, and she was well prepared to speak. "To a world very much needing his character, his gifts, and his love for Christ, we proudly and humbly release Kirk to adulthood," she read. "We know him to be steadfast, strong, and true. We love you so much, Kirk; you've been an incredible blessing. We release you to the target of being all you can be in Christ. Thank you for having graced our lives with your remarkable sonship."

Then Karen quoted from the Old Testament: "So be strong, show yourself a man, and observe what the LORD your God requires: Walk in his ways, and keep his decrees and commands, his laws and requirements, as written in the Law of Moses, so that you may prosper in all you do and wherever you go, and that the LORD may keep his promise to me" (1 Kings 2:2-4, NIV).

She concluded with a short passage from Corinthians: "Be on your guard; stand firm in the faith; be [a man] of courage; be strong. Do everything in love" (1 Cor. 16:13, NIV).

God's Word hung in the air between us: strong, true, and directive; challenging and affirming; a signpost as clear as if the Lord was standing right there, reading the text out loud.

One of the servers could not stop herself from jumping in. "You guys have always been my role models," she said. "I look up to you all; I'm going to miss you so much."

Meg, fifteen, could not hold back her tears. "I've always wanted to be just like you," she said. "I don't know what I will do when you are gone. You are the best people in the world!"

I watched these wonderful young people with their strong, loving parents, and I listened carefully. I wondered about the kinds of tools necessary to even attempt the amazing achievement all those families had pulled off. How had it happened? Was it all haphazard? Were they just lucky? Or, is there something to learn about being deliberate, about being strategic in our approach to a distinctive Christian pilgrimage?

There was something powerful in that room. The parents had great raw material to work with, but they also had employed God's everlasting Word to equip these graduates for their journey. This was more than just a transition from high school to college; it was a commissioning to the great pilgrim adventure.

The guide book

All the best trips come with some kind of guide: a travel book, a AAA planning map, a person, interpretive material—sometimes all of the above. In my family it has always been my wife, Rebekah. She researches; she stocks up on brochures and magazines; she even reads relevant novels ahead of time (*Bury My Heart at Wounded Knee* just before our epic trip out West; *The Call of the Wild* when we were getting ready for Alaska; *All Creatures Great and Small* to prepare for a holiday in Yorkshire, England; always deep background).

When we took our family to see America's Civil War battle-fields, we were the parents who made our children watch the entire twelve-week PBS documentary series before we even rolled out of our driveway. Friday nights: pizza, popcorn, and Ken Burns.

Then we traveled the opposite direction for the all-important three-week "Heritage Trip" to England. We joined the National Trust, took the *English Heritage* magazine, and then toured as people who actually knew something. We had a book with the historical details of every single community in the U.K.; we could stop in the village green, walk into the parish church, and always know what we were looking at.

I sometimes suspect Rebekah took all those college classes in art history and the humanities just in case she had kids one day.

Likewise, our journey as pilgrims comes equipped with the best-ever printed guide, God's Word. I remember the ditty my friends and I memorized in Sunday school: "The best book to read is the Bible; the best book to read is the Bible. If we read it every day, it will guide us on our way. Oh! The best book to read is the Bible."

Five thousand miles away, Rebekah grew up in Georgia and then Florida. She may have lived in a different universe, but she got exactly the same message, loud and clear. God's Word took center stage, and she sang about it in Sunday school with all her heart. "The B-I-B-L-E. Yes, that's the book for me. I stand alone on the Word of God; the B-I-B-L-E!"

We memorized these classic songs well before we could even read. God's Word is an indispensable resource on my journey; without it, without a deep searching knowledge that builds over time, I would be like one of those tourists who breezes through Europe barely scratching the surface, sending postcards to friends featuring messages like:

"If it's Tuesday, it must be Paris. . . ."

"This afternoon we spent almost a whole day in London. . . ." and,

"The Scottish Highlands are spectacular; a day and a half on the bus, and there's pretty much nothing left to see. . . ."

Billy Graham

I must have been eleven years old when my family made the trek into London to hear Billy Graham preach his 1967 crusade at one of the great exhibition halls. I remember standing on the sidewalk with crowds of people waiting to get in. I remember listening to George Beverly Shea sing "How Great Thou Art" with a voice that reached deep and true. I remember Billy Graham himself, pencil thin in a dark suit, peppering his message with this singular phrase, "The Bible says," time and again, offering God with a clarity that was at once comforting and penetrating, reassuring and incisive.

It wasn't the crowds; it wasn't the preacher's charismatic presentation—in truth there was nothing remarkable at all about the man himself—and it wasn't even the inspirational music or the emotion of the occasion that worked on my heart in such a compelling fashion. Instead, I was captured by the simple power resident in God's Word. I was listening to the Bible; I wasn't distracted; and the message was crystal clear. That's the authority that impressed me so much that I simply had to go forward and make a decision to follow Christ.

Billy Graham quoted the text—the King James Version in that day—from heart: "And these are they which are sown among thorns; such as hear the word, and the cares of this world, and the deceitfulness of riches, and the lusts of other things entering in, choke the word, and it becometh unfruitful" (Mark 4:18-19).

The NRSV uses the following translation for verse 19: "The cares of the world, and the lure of wealth, and the desire for other things come in and choke the word, and it yields nothing."

I'd been distracted by these "other things," and I knew it. The words rang true. Today, too often, I'm distracted still. But Billy Graham taught me that God's awesome power and purpose are living and present in God's Word—spoken aloud or captured in the heart—preserved in the text of the Holy Bible.

I made my way to the front of the auditorium, and I declared my intention to follow Jesus. There I met a counselor by the name of Norman Lynn. Mr. Lynn prayed with me, talked with me, and continued to speak God's Word to my receptive heart. He gave me some literature, and he promised to follow up.

Norman Lynn was as good as his word. He talked with my parents; he communicated with my pastor; and he wrote me a long letter just a few days after the crusade. Then—and this is hard to believe but it speaks to how faithful the man was—he continued to correspond with me on a regular basis. He asked hard questions, pointed me back to scripture, and celebrated when I was baptized. He sent me postcards from vacation; he commiserated with me when my favorite soccer team did poorly; and he continually followed through on his pledge to be a part of my ongoing spiritual journey.

"Don't ever get too far away from the Word of God," he told me on more than one occasion. "Yes, it's the best book there is; and yes, it's inspirational. But it's so much more; the Bible is my daily guide."

Norman Lynn didn't follow through for just a few weeks or just a few months. My Billy Graham Crusade counselor stayed in close contact until a few weeks before my wedding—five thousand miles away in America—twelve years down the road—and he ended his follow-through by writing a wonderful letter to my wife-to-be. He told Rebekah that he was "handing off" responsibility for my spiritual life and nurture to her. He also assured her that his deep and faithful commitment to prayer would never waver until the day he passed into glory.

"Rebekah," he wrote, "I pass on to you the spiritual nurture of my brother Derek. May God bless you both." He passed away not long after the wedding. Maybe that's why Rebekah went on to complete her seminary education; she knew what a Herculean task she had in store.

Family devotions

It was no accident then that Rebekah and I decided we shouldn't even think about raising our own family without rooting and grounding our children in the power and truth of scripture from day one. Church is great; Sunday school is nice; Wednesday programs are well and fine; small-group and fellowship experiences are a huge piece of the puzzle. Investing ourselves in the church family does so much to round out a spiritual life. But none of the above even comes close to making up for the most important element ever conceived when it comes to foundational training in matters of faith. I'm talking about family devotions. A family that reads God's Word and prays together on a daily basis is the absolute best launching ground for the pilgrim path.

Let me repeat that: the family that reads God's Word and prays together on a daily basis is the absolute best launching ground for the pilgrim path.

Rebekah and I chose the dinner hour. We made a commitment to eat together—as a family—at least five days every week, and we always concluded the meal with Bible reading and prayer. Those times together were—and sometimes still are—an oasis in the spiritual wilderness even the strongest families often negotiate from day to day.

"But you don't understand," so many of our peers told us, "It's not easy, and there are so many competing activities."

Granted. But last time I looked, it still takes the earth twenty-four hours to rotate on its axis and a little more than 365 days to transcribe its journey around the sun. That's true if we live in

Tampa, New York, London, Paris, or Istanbul. The Bible tells us that the sun shines—or the rain falls—or something like that—on both the just and the unjust (Matt. 5:45). At the end of the day—and that's a twenty-four-hour day—your family or my family has either made the choice to be grounded in God's Word and the fellowship of prayer—or we have made the choice not to.

Our faith journey is no pilgrimage in any sense of the word outside of our intention to lean on the power and the promises of God's extraordinary Word. It's not a journey to somewhere if it doesn't involve leaving other things behind. It's the pilgrim path, and it's certainly not a walk in the park.

I was especially interested when I discovered studies (information compiled at www.togetherfordinner.com) that documented a strong correlation between regular family mealtimes and the health of children across the board, but I wasn't the least bit surprised. Listen to the following words that God delivered to his children when they were pilgrims in a literal wilderness:

> Hear, O Israel: The LORD is our God, the LORD alone. You shall love the LORD your God with all your heart, and with all your soul, and with all your might. Keep these words that I am commanding you today in your heart. Recite them to your children and talk about them when you are at home and when you are away, when you lie down and when you rise. Bind them as a sign on your hand, fix them as an emblem on your forehead, and write them on the doorposts of your house and on your gates.—Deuteronomy 6:4-9

Columbine High School

We all remember the terrible day in 1999 when two heavily armed teens systematically mowed down their high-school classmates in a Colorado school. The event sent shock waves throughout the nation.

The following weekend my adult Sunday school class simply couldn't get going. We opened with prayer but then just sat there, morose, talking about the tragedy and bemoaning our impotence when it came to doing anything at all to help. About twenty-five of us, mostly parents of teens ourselves, sat in a semicircle. "What's the absolute worst about it is that I have no idea what to do," one class member said. "I just feel so helpless—and hopeless."

Our room has a massive set of picture windows with a view over a kind of quad. At the precise moment those words of hopelessness were uttered, as if released by our voices, the doors from the youth house burst open, and around thirty scruffy teens spilled out over the patio.

They made their way across the space, moving en masse in front of our window, tumbling on and around the sidewalk, tousling one another like puppies, laughing and yelling in a beautiful mob of irrepressible life. They were on their way to the sanctuary, getting ready to rehearse skits, readings, and music for the upcoming Youth Sunday, a day when the whole scraggly bunch of them would lead the rest of us through what has come to be known—affectionately—as "the fastest hour in worship."

I looked around the room. My adult class members were all mesmerized. Tears rolled down several faces. Mouths literally hung open. I knew exactly what they were thinking.

Although I didn't need to say it, I couldn't help myself. "Can you look out of that window and still say there's nothing we can do in the face of such apparent hopelessness as the massacre this week at Columbine?" I asked. "I'd say we're already doing it. I'd say we're launching some amazing new pilgrims into a life of discipleship. And I'd say that our young people are armed with God's truth rather than automatic weapons. They are packing love instead of hate, moving with purpose rather than being stymied by purposelessness. I'd say we're doing a lot."

———

Before we knew it, close to a decade had passed. It's now 2008, and I'm sitting in that same room, eating dinner and celebrating with yet another group of high-school graduates. Beautiful, talented, restless, and eager to get on with this life, a life they feel ready to grab hold of with both hands. This set of children was around nine years old, probably enrolled in the third grade, when the Columbine tragedy made their parents so sad.

Once again parents stand, and intimate stories are shared. Hearts are poured out, faith is expressed. There is laughter, and there are tears. But this time I have a few words too. You see, I've been thinking a great deal about this pilgrim path we're all taking, and I want to say something to the young people and their families that will encourage them in their commitment to be deliberate followers of Jesus, pilgrims in progress.

"It may be a cliché to say that it's a great big world out there," I began. "But fact is it's not the world you've been raised with. It's not the world you've experienced here in this loving church around people who nurture and love you unconditionally. This world is— and we can't forget this—the same world that God loves dearly, and this world is exactly the place where he purposes for each one of us to shine."

Most people go on way too long at such events, talking well beyond the attention span of a late evening, so I grabbed my Bible, turned to one of my favorite passages, and cut to the chase. "The apostle Paul is encouraging each one of us to live," I said, "as 'children of God without blemish in the midst of a crooked and perverse generation, in which you shine like stars in the world' (Phil. 2:15).

"Paul goes on to say that there's really only one context in which he could possibly boast, that would demonstrate that he hadn't been involved in their lives for nothing," I continued, "and

I'd like to endorse his point with every possible emphasis this fine evening. Here it is, just a phrase. Listen: 'It is by your holding fast to the word of life that I can boast'" (Phil. 2:16).

I looked each young person in the eye, spoke his or her name, and repeated the powerful words: Hold fast to the word of life. Hold fast to the word of life. Hold fast to the word of life. Hold fast to the word of life.

Questions for Reflection

1. When have you felt the pilgrim path was too big a challenge, beyond your ability to navigate on your own?
2. How often do you read the Bible? Is your commitment to God's word regular or haphazard?
3. Consider the potential for healing when we allow ourselves to be saturated with God's voice through scripture.

What is your favorite Bible verse? Has your favorite passage changed over time? Do new verses capture you sometimes? Share your favorite scripture at www.part-time-christian.blogspot.com/

Prayer

Help us to remember the awesome power resident in your Word, gracious God. We cannot journey effectively outside the encouragement and the accountability present in every text. Amen.

ten

A Collision
of Worlds

The true light, which enlightens everyone, was coming into the
world. He was in the world, and the world came into being
through him; yet the world did not know him.—John 1:9-10

Sometimes we struggle. This pilgrim path, it seems at times, runs
contrary to the rules and the limitations of the world we are used to.

I got up to walk the dog today, bright and early at 6:30 AM. I witnessed the beginning of a beautiful clear January morning and
enjoyed the glory of God's good creation. It felt refreshing to be
outside, breathing in the clean air, offering the coming hours to
Jesus, engaging the promise of a new day.

At the same time, it was impossible to crowd out the commitments, the conflict, the discord, the busyness, the sickness, and
the disappointment that are all vying for attention inside my head
and down into my soul. We live in a broken world. That's a given,

and sometimes it brushes up against me in a harsh way. It's then that I struggle.

At the beginning of the Bible we read an astounding claim about the true nature of people: "Then God said, 'Let us make humankind in our image, according to our likeness'" (Gen. 1:26).

People: human beings, men and women, we are revealed by history as deeply flawed and tragically broken, yet at the same time created in the image of God.

God: by definition perfect, is revealed by history as deeply loving and interested in a relationship with people, yet at the same time faultless and just in every way.

Earth: finite, temporary, corrupt, worn, spoiled; limited by time and space.

Then there is God's kingdom: infinite and redemptive, beyond description or measurement.

All of us—women and men—are created beings equipped with brains that begin to atrophy many years before we really learn how to use them. God—in stark contrast—owns the capacity to hold and guard all knowledge, create new knowledge, and love profoundly each intimate detail of creation. Are we getting a clear picture? Does the built-in logical contradiction of the idea "Let us make humankind in our image, according to our likeness . . ." trouble us at all?

With these thoughts in mind, let's talk about a concept we call *dissonance*.

- Dissonance is the grating together of apparently incompatible realities.
- It's God playing an A-major concerto while I join in via badly tuned strings in the key of F-minus flat—sometimes F-minus flat out of tune.
- It's the screech of invective in the middle of a conversation about peace.

- It's the chronic misreading of Jesus in a world that needs to understand the real and interactive meaning of God's love.
- It's "Blessed are the meek" when the standards that define success in human terms require dominance and profit at the expense of others.
- Dissonance is, mostly, exactly where we live.

God breaking in

My friends Carolyn and Stan have three very cool children—all boys. Mike, the oldest, had a rough experience making it safely into this life from the moment he made his debut. His parents thought they were going to lose him before they even knew him. He almost died more than once, stayed in the hospital a long time; and it was a miracle that he was eventually able to go home. Fast-forward to an early family Christmas in Carolyn and Stan's home; Mike is a preschooler.

"We were setting out the manger scene," Carolyn remembers. "Putting everything in place and telling the story. Mike was old enough to start getting some details, and so I picked up the figure of Jesus and put it in his hand."

My friend made sure she had her son's complete attention.

"Do you know who this is, Mike?" Carolyn asked. "This is the baby Jesus."

"Oh, I know Jesus," Mike said, enthusiastically. "Jesus came to visit me when I was in the hospital. But he didn't look so much like a baby then."

A few years ago, my friend Susan's mother was dangerously ill; she went through two serious cancer surgeries over the course of just a few weeks. Susan knew that people were praying, and knowing that fact gave her real strength. Susan's family was supportive, plus her mother was part of a vital and caring faith community.

"People are praying around the clock," Susan told me and Rebekah; "But she'd appreciate the addition of your prayers too."

"Certainly," we said. "We promise we'll pray."

A few days later, my wife called Susan to ask about her mother. "I was praying for your mother yesterday evening," Rebekah said.

"You say you prayed for her?" Susan replied as a question; there was more than normal interest in her voice. "You didn't stop by the hospital and pray with my mom?"

"No," Rebekah told her, "there wasn't time to go out to the hospital yesterday. So I simply opened my heart, and I prayed. I was either at the office or working at home the whole day."

There was a long silence, and Rebekah wondered if she had possibly said something wrong.

"That's really remarkable." Susan eventually continued. "But now I'm curious; exactly what time did you pray for my mom?"

"Around seven," Rebekah said. "Why?"

She could hear the tears creeping in amongst Susan's words. "Mom called me this morning," she said. "Yesterday had been a very hard day, and she had needed some extra comfort. She told me, 'I had a wonderful visit from Rebekah Maul yesterday evening. She was so very kind, and she prayed with me.'

"Rebekah, Mom has been a little out of it with all the medication she's taking, but she was very clear about last night. It would have been exactly the time that you were on your knees."

Susan's mother has only met Rebekah a handful of times, and Susan hadn't mentioned Rebekah by name in weeks. It might have been easier to explain if she'd dreamed about her pastor stopping by or maybe another friend from her church. But, no, it was Rebekah—the same Rebekah who happened to be on her knees at that precise moment and who ministered directly to her spirit that evening; Rebekah, a pilgrim in progress who had given herself to the discipline of purposeful prayer.

I have no idea how the mechanics of prayer work, and I'm fairly confident I never will. I have no idea exactly how God uses us or precisely what forces God sets in motion when we own the truth of being made in the image of our Creator and choose to completely submit to God's guidance. I'm simply privileged, sometimes, to be a witness to some powerful examples.

Non sequitur

What we're talking about here is a kind of dissonance. It's the conflict between realities. We live in this temporal world, yet we are eternal in our nature. We inhabit bodies that are fragile and seriously flawed, yet we are also children of the most high God, and we are invited to live redeemed lives of victory and great purpose. "Blessed are the poor in spirit," Jesus said, "for theirs is the kingdom of heaven" (Matt. 5:3).

In the book of Ecclesiastes, the Teacher put it this way: "I have seen the business that God has given to everyone to be busy with. He has made everything suitable for its time; moreover he has put a sense of past and future into their minds, yet they cannot find out what God has done from the beginning to the end" (Eccles. 3:10-11).

Eternity is set deep in hearts that live out physical lives in the here and now. But eternity in a sense is the here and now; at least that's where time without end begins. The pilgrim must learn to tell time in both realities. God's time is at once beautiful and challenging. But this is not an observation that causes disharmony so much as it is a perspective we can learn to appreciate. "I have said this to you, so that in me you may have peace. In the world you face persecution [trouble, dissonance]. But take courage; I have conquered [overcome] the world!" (John 16:33).

Otherworldly

Many mythologies offer stories to explain the interaction between the mortal world and the spiritual realm, or the dividing line that marks the borders of these realms. These stories explore the juxtaposition between that which is eternal and our flesh-and-blood experience on this terrestrial plane. The meeting place—or separation point—between the human and the divine is sometimes described as a "membrane." At certain times and places, such traditions say, the membrane is stretched thin, and communication between separate worlds is most likely to take place.

In a move that went a step further even than mythology could imagine, God actually entered time and space in the person of Jesus. Then—now—this God Immanuel offers the Christ-life to his followers. Today Jesus invites us to live the reality of kingdom life. "I am the gate," Jesus said. "Whoever enters by me will be saved, and will come in and go out and find pasture" (John 10:9).

I am the entry point, the way in, the place where the membrane is stretched to invisibility, Jesus is telling us, *people come in, and they go out.* We become in a sense otherworldly. We experience a paradigm shift, and we live out of this new reality—a kingdom mentality.

So there is going to be conflict; there is going to be grating; there is going to be a shift from the patterns of living that define this fallen, broken, sphere. There is going to be dissonance. And—as pilgrims in progress—we can expect to experience more than a little dissonance to the extent that we live authentic kingdom lives.

Pharisees and other hypocrites

Modern-day Christians love to give the Pharisees of Christ's time a bad rap. It's a kind of sport: Pin the Criticism on the Pharisee! However, in trying to lay out distinctions between a social/cultural

Christian and an honest-to-God Jesus follower, I've got to say we all have something to learn from the friendly neighborhood Pharisee.

"But come on," you say. "Jesus was calling those guys hypocrites all the time. Surely they're fair game?"

First, Jesus was illustrating a point. Second, it's a safe bet to suggest that Jesus might well label a few of us frauds too.

Pharisees played an important role in the Hebrew world, helping guard the "special-ness" of what it meant to be God's chosen people. Being chosen is not only a privilege; it amounts to an enormous responsibility. To be honest, the Israelites weren't always up to being that special as a people; sometimes they just wanted to blend in.

Take a look at the following exchange between the children of Israel and the (long-suffering) prophet Samuel. Israel was refusing to listen to Samuel's insistence that they guard their identity. "No!" Israel said, "but we are determined to have a king over us, so that we also may be like other nations" (1 Sam. 8:19-20).

The children of Israel constantly struggle to maintain the uniqueness of their faith—worshiping one God and actually living like a bona fide chosen nation. The average temple-going Israelite constantly slid backward and sideways into being just "like the other nations." The danger was that there would be nothing unique about the Hebrew people anymore, nothing to set them apart and communicate God's faithful covenant to the world.

So it was up to the Pharisees to help. *No, that's not what it means to be God's chosen people,* they'd say; *it looks like this . . . it looks like this . . . it looks like this. Let's talk about it. Let's read the scriptures together. Let's get it right.*

Dissonance is a difficult place to be. We don't like eternal principles to chafe so obviously against the comfort of familiarity; we don't like the tension one bit. Dissonance grates on our nerves; we want it to resolve.

A long way east of Eden

The pilgrim way is like a new tune for God's people. It's a song that finds its genesis in the word God spoke to declare our very creation—your creation and mine—before the dawn of time. Jesus had a catchphrase: "Seek first God's kingdom."

Such an approach, the Savior pointed out, does not register in the same key the people typically were singing there around Galilee, in the public square, here in North America—a long way east of Eden. The kingdom path is at odds with the road map produced by other contenders for our allegiance.

But Jesus said, "Seek. . . ."

The Master did not say, *First earn your way into God's kingdom; meet me there and then we'll talk.* Instead the Lord said, "Seek." "But seek his kingdom, and these things will be given to you as well" (Luke 12:31, NIV).

We are tempted to look for quick resolution and to end the dissonance via the path of least resistance: *Just let me be like all the other nations, Lord; let me be just like everyone else.* Then things will be okay.

Well, no.

Jesus has promised us admission into this kingdom life that we seek. No pressure, no results-oriented demands; just process, journey, pilgrim path. "Do not be afraid, little flock," Jesus continued by way of promise in Luke 12:32 (NIV), "for your Father has been pleased to give you the kingdom."

The kingdom is already ours. So why the dissonance? We're singing this song in a broken world that's not getting fixed overnight. That's one reason it is vital to have friends with us as we move beyond part-time faith, people to sing along, people to harmonize, people to help keep us well tuned, people to keep us grounded.

Meanwhile, the entire created order is anxious to hear us sing God's redemption song. "For the creation waits with eager longing

for the revealing of the children of God; for the creation was subjected to futility, not of its own will but by the will of the one who
subjected it, in hope that the creation itself will be set free from its
bondage to decay and will obtain the freedom of the glory of the
children of God" (Rom. 8:19-21).

God turns it all over

Word of caution: following Jesus full tilt can leave us breathless,
stretched to capacity, almost a little unnerved. This pilgrimage is
going to require courage, but it is a journey that is 100 percent necessary if we are going to be revealed as the children of God and if
we are ever going to help set this creation free from its bondage
and decay.

Jesus is in the world, certainly working in and through many
faithful disciples, and though the world does not know the Son
(John 1:9-10), it remains God's intention that those of us who are
committed to being "pilgrims in progress" step up to make the
introductions.

The light of the world will make the truth clear to everyone;
that's part of the purpose behind this pilgrim path. That's why we
choose—every day—to follow Jesus.

Questions for Reflection

1. In what way has your pilgrim way moved close to being "otherworldly"?
2. Does the dissonance between kingdom life and the world we
inhabit unnerve you? Or are you intrigued by the journey?
3. Describe how a more predictable life of faith would make
you more comfortable. But, be honest, if following Jesus was
less challenging, wouldn't you miss the sense of adventure?

4. Think seriously about asking the Holy Spirit to be a more active guide along the path.
5. Does Jesus ever unnerve you? How do you react when that happens?

Talk about Jesus pushing the edge of your comfort zone at
www.part-time-christian.blogspot.com/

Prayer

We have to confess, Lord, that normal and run of the mill have a lot of appeal at times. We're not always ready for Jesus to rock our boat. So rock us gently, gracious God, but not too gently, and grant us the courage to enter into the spirit of your revolution. Amen.

eleven

Where Grace Shatters Darkness

You are the light of the world. A city built on a hill cannot be hid. No one after lighting a lamp puts it under the bushel basket, but on the lampstand, and it gives light to all in the house. In the same way, let your light shine before others, so that they may see your good works and give glory to your Father in heaven.—Matthew 5:14-16

World War II

My mother lived in East London at the onset of World War II. England declared war on Germany on September 3, 1939. The government quickly implemented emergency plans to evacuate the nation's children from danger zones all across the south. Not only were bombs beginning to fall from the sky, but the threat of invasion was both imminent and real. Once the British army was defeated at Dunkirk in June of 1940, massive landings by German troops were expected almost immediately.

Winston Churchill is well remembered for his "We shall fight on the beaches" speech (June 4, 1940). Many people forget that the indefatigable prime minister was not simply employing rhetoric. Churchill believed his countrymen and women would be fighting invading forces on the beaches maybe within the hour, possibly tomorrow morning, probably next week, certainly within the month.

Consequently, children of all ages were moved out of London and the southeastern counties. They were sent away as entire schools, teachers included. My dad was eleven when he boarded a train to take him to safety, and his parents didn't know where he was going. His school arrived at a town in northern England several hours later. The children were picked over by local people instructed to select one or two children each. He ended up living in a pub, separated from his sisters. My grandparents learned their children's addresses only after David, Margaret, and Gladys dutifully wrote letters home. He was gone the best part of four years.

My mother, Grace Kemp, was eight when hostilities erupted into war. She didn't stay away so long. Sent to live with relatives in the country, she didn't last the duration. She returned to London after a year because "if my mum and dad were going to be killed with a bomb, then I decided I wanted to be with them."

It turns out the entire family almost were killed one day when a huge explosion leveled several homes in their block. My mother's part of London endured constant strafing and bombing. Later in the conflict, the dreaded buzz bombs started to drop in random patterns. Also known as the V-1 or doodlebug, the heinous unguided missiles were filled with just enough fuel to make the flight from the European continent. Then, depending on a number of variables, including wind direction and quality of fuel, the noisy devices would run out of gas. Their engines shut off without warning, and the bombs would fall like death from the sky in the menacing silence.

My granddad built a shelter in the back garden, a place of questionable safety, where the family would often spend the night. As the bombs fell—both conventional ordnance from Luftwaffe bombers and the buzz bombs—my grandmother would read the psalms aloud (my mother especially remembers Psalm 46:1: "God is our refuge and strength" and Psalm 91:1: "He that dwelleth in the secret place of the most High shall abide under the shadow of the Almighty," KJV). She said the family felt an uncommon measure of peace.

There were close calls, and then there were closer calls.

One day, standing just outside the kitchen door, my mother was listening and watching as another V-1 traced its way across the sky. The buzz bombs flew low enough to be seen. Suddenly the engine cut out, and my granddad quickly calculated its lethal trajectory.

"Get into the shelter!" he yelled, literally shoving his family through the door.

The bomb hit directly across the street, completely demolishing three adjacent homes. At my mother's house, every window and door was blown out; every ceiling came crashing down; every piece of glass was shattered (she said the walls were pitted with shards like darts in a dartboard). The dining room table was thrown across the living room, almost crushing the kitchen wall. My uncle, caught upstairs, miraculously escaped injury. Their next-door neighbor was standing in his front entry where the door killed him instantly, like a missile launched from a gun.

Enough children had returned to my mother's suburb by the early 1940s to warrant a functioning local school. The rule, she said, was that if she heard an air-raid warning less than halfway to the school, she should run home; if she had passed that mark, she was supposed to seek shelter at the school. "Sometimes I'd be just outside the school gate," she smiled, "but if I heard the siren before my foot touched the playground, I'd turn around and run all the way home."

When victory in Europe was declared, my mother's church started a ministry to German prisoners of war. Members sponsored a Sunday-afternoon reception every week at a camp nearby, providing tea and snacks even though strict rationing remained in place for several more years. Grace Kemp's family made some firm friendships. One young soldier, Gunter, found a special place in their hearts. It didn't matter that just a short while previous huge German bombs had destroyed much of the neighborhood; it didn't count that my mother's home had been smashed to smithereens; and the family didn't hold it against the German soldiers that my granddad's reconstruction work had been so intense and so overwhelming that he had suffered a complete breakdown the previous year.

What did matter was grace. Grace is an unmerited free gift. My mother's church extended grace because they knew Jesus, and they followed in the pilgrim way of Christlike love. My mother extended grace because she already knew it by heart.

Gunter, my mother's new friend, was eventually repatriated, but he was disappointed to discover his hometown by then firmly behind the Iron Curtain. He and my mother lost touch; he could not travel, and long years rolled by.

A lifetime later, the work of providence and grace brought them together again. Almost five decades had passed when, after the 1989 demolition of the Berlin Wall, my mother, along with my dad, was finally able to visit her old friend.

"I never knew what real love was," Gunter told them, "until those days after the war when your church reached out with God's unconditional love to me and to the other soldiers."

The quality of love the young German experienced in my mother's postwar London is a key ingredient of grace. Grace is active, insistent. It is countercultural, and it is difficult to understand. Grace does not allow evil to dictate the boundaries of its expression; instead, it gets up and does something that makes a lifetime of difference—usually something costly.

It seems that our world is always at war. I wonder what those of us who seek to make our way along the pilgrim road can do today to lead our neighbors into such a journey of grace. "The light shines in the darkness, but the darkness has not understood it" (John 1:5, NIV).

Grace is the antidote to darkness

If grace was at work in my mother's London, then grace certainly propelled Europe toward daylight in the sixteenth century. Both Renaissance and Reformation are best understood in terms of emergent light and insistent grace. Redemption broke in to help end an eon of little light and even less understanding about how Jesus can radically transform common life and infuse it with possibility.

To move beyond being a part-time Christian is to move into light. Enlightenment engages the spirit because God is the source of light and life. Darkness is always threatened by progress. We don't get rewarded for doing life right; it's not a game, not a puzzle, not a contest. And God does not punish us—most fortunate for me—when we get things wrong.

We're not on this road hoping to find Jesus; we're on this road with Jesus as our companion and our guide. We're not figuring things out so we can stumble onto God; we're struggling along because we already have. And when we run into opposition, we don't take up arms and slug it out in order to gain a yard or two for our beleaguered deity; far from it, we simply and deliberately participate in the victory that has already been secured.

Grace puts me in a headlock

In my own experience, maybe due to natural stubbornness, the understanding that I am helpless outside the initiatives of grace is a lesson continually in the making. Each mileage marker on this pilgrim path is another point where I pause, once again aware of the truth of it. Indeed, I cannot move forward in any other way.

This is God's craft with me. By grace the Creator draws me in.

There are times in my journey as a pilgrim when the truth about the way that God loves me is found in the struggle, the wrestling, the brokenness, and the holding close. In fact, I am convinced the journey demands that I—like Jacob—at times tussle with God (Gen. 32:22-32).

God's best; no half measures

Too often I duck the opportunity, avoiding the call to take the Lord's invitation seriously. We all hold back and squander precious time. God constantly nudges, coaching and encouraging, and I wonder why we settle for less than our Creator's best.

What does it mean for a pilgrim to journey with enthusiasm? How does "live as if we mean it" translate into our life of faith, our Christian witness, and our jobs as teachers, managers, ministers, lawyers, sales reps, homemakers, students, sales assistants, nurses, and so on?

When my mother's church stepped outside the darkness of WWII and acted with the Christ-life in transformational grace, they modeled light beyond any words that could be spoken. All for Jesus. No half measures and no holding back. Half measures are thoroughly incompatible with our identity as disciples. Each moment marks new opportunity, as Jesus followers, to add salt and light to a world anxious for redemption.

Never has this principle come into clearer focus than when I worked as a school teacher. I'd always insisted that teaching was the last thing I'd ever do for work, but the Author of Life had other plans. Because God designed me with specific purposes in mind, God understands perfectly where my gifts find best expression— even if it takes a few years of finessing and fine-tuning to hone the original raw material. God knew where this pilgrimage would lead me if only I dared to continue forward progress, if only I would put one foot in front of the other and let the Spirit be my guide.

A return to the Dark Ages

My teaching career started in a mental health day treatment program, a creative model in which the local school system worked in collaboration with community agencies. Later I took a job working with at-risk students in a large middle school. The students in my classroom, aged eleven to fourteen, all had been labeled emotionally handicapped. It was a catchall designation that included, essentially, any child who failed to learn because his or her behavior got in the way.

I taught social studies and language arts, but mostly I taught behavior management. It's just about impossible for children to learn—and I still believe this—when they are acting out or are out of balance emotionally.

My middle-school experience got under way in early October, when I was hired to replace the third teacher in as many weeks who had resigned in frustration or fear or both. This was, in every respect, a hard assignment:

- The classroom was a decrepit portable sitting on the edge of campus.
- The students had racked up numerous suspensions (the previous teachers had sent—on average—six students per day to

the dean's office because they couldn't handle such creatively troublesome behaviors).

- The textbooks were out of date and in poor condition.
- The students had been written off by the administration.
- The number one job, according to the principal: "Keep those hooligans out of sight, and make sure they don't bother the rest of us."

My first day on board I was asked to introduce myself at the morning staff meeting. My words were brief and to the point. "Glad to meet you all," I said. "My name is Derek Maul. I have a request for those who pray: please do."

I made good progress in short order. I ran a tight ship, and I didn't run crying to the administration. The young people were glad to be in a situation where they knew what to expect. Once the disruptive behaviors settled down, I had to confront the colossal gap in knowledge these students had amassed over time. Their ignorance was like a deep moat; it not only cut them off from opportunity but isolated them from just about everything in a debilitating fashion.

One day the real cost of cultivated mediocrity became so clear to me that I confronted it head-on. We were getting ready to talk about some of the early explorers—people like Marco Polo, Vasco da Gama, and Columbus. I wanted to set the stage and help my students see why the Europeans were crossing continents, boarding boats, and heading into the frightening unknown—why they were beginning to discover their world.

Naturally, we started talking about the Enlightenment and Renaissance—that period of history when it began to dawn on more and more people that learning, art, creativity, beauty, expression, and mobility were all possible; that lives could begin to move beyond the restrictive parameters that contained them; that freedom from the tyranny of ignorance was even conceivable.

By logical extension, no interpretation of Enlightenment is possible without understanding the long darkness that preceded it. So we developed an outline of some of the conditions that characterized the Dark Ages.

We talked about the absence of education, institutionalized ignorance, the fact that few people traveled more than a handful of miles from their homes, the lack of worldview, and what it meant to live lives predetermined from birth to eke out a limited existence based on social position. We covered nonparticipation in government, absent or undiscovered creative skills, overwhelming poverty, and the consummate inability of folk to conceive of anything other than the narrow life they were living.

That's when I noticed myself begin to get angry. My heart started to burn, and it was all I could do not to preach at my young charges. You see it dawned on me, right there in the middle of fourth-period social studies, that this was exactly where so many of my students' lives were heading. They were embarked on a voluntary return to the Dark Ages—and it just about made me sick.

Here is a sampling of what my students were saying:

"I don't need to learn no math 'cause I'm out of school first chance I get, picking up my money on the street."

"My boyfriend and me gonna get a baby and get us a government check. That's how we gonna live."

"Got my homey here do all my readin' for me."

"You know nothin's gonna change, man. So why even bother?"

"Do you know what you're doing?" I almost shouted at the class. They had the idea that something had worked its way under my skin, and I could see them glancing around, wondering who was in trouble.

"It took the European continent hundreds of years to claw its way out of the Dark Ages," I upped my decibels a notch or two. "The United States was founded because our ancestors believed that there was something else possible for them. The ideas that shaped the Declaration of Independence and the Constitution were a natural result of the movement of thought and action away from tyranny and ignorance and fear. This country emerged as the high-water mark of renaissance in thought, government, and religious freedom."

I took a deep breath. A few of my students had started to look interested—if only because they thought maybe their teacher had lost his mind. But I was a long way from reaching the majority.

"Excuse me," I said, and ran out of the classroom. When I returned I was pushing an abandoned shopping cart someone had rolled on campus that morning.

"Take a good look," I said, kicking it across the front of the room, where it crashed heavily into a student's desk. "We might as well put a sign on the front that says WELCOME BACK TO THE DARK AGES. Because a lot of you are going to be pushing these around town for a living if you don't start believing that it's worthwhile to learn something soon."

Now I had their attention.

"It may have taken Europe hundreds of years to climb out of the Dark Ages, but listen to this: each human being who willingly chooses ignorance over learning, who allows the circumstances of birth to limit the potential of life, who rejects reading and creativity, and who refuses to participate in freedom and democracy— each one of you who goes down that road is choosing a fast return to the Dark Ages—with about three years of effort . . ." And then the bell rang.

We tried to pick up the discussion the next day, but it was difficult because some parent had complained that I had called her child ignorant. "School's meant to be building my boy up," one mother lectured the principal. "Tell him he's somebody. I think that teacher needs to watch his mouth."

Later I published a commentary on the incident in the Tampa *Tribune*, noting how easily we set aside the ideals that defined our emergence from medieval feudalism. It is disturbing to witness citizens of a free country return to ignorance and fear; to watch children see their future as immutably cast, without possibility of change; to observe an elective return to darkness.

Desperation has taken over too many vulnerable minds, and it is a short walk from desperation to the end of hope, and from the end of hope to the end of real living.

The challenge to live

We have this huge opportunity as Jesus followers: we can apply *grace, renaissance,* and *enlightenment* to our Christian witness. There is no light without gospel; there is no renaissance without the Spirit; there is no real enlightenment without, also, reformation.

Does our discipleship sparkle in a way that might attract others to join us? Or do we stumble along; head down, shoulders slumped, shuffling our feet?

Do people see Christ followers as the kind of inspirational witnesses Jesus imagined? "Let your light shine before others, so that they may see your good works and give glory to your Father in heaven" (Matt. 5:16).

Are we committed to presenting Jesus to our world? Are we the presence of Christ in and through all that we do?

Does our path as pilgrims represent the consummate cure for mediocrity?

Here's an interesting footnote: my mother's church community called themselves "The Peculiar People." They considered themselves qualitatively different because they followed Jesus, and they expected to behave as radical Jesus followers, most unlike the world around them.

Full-time Christians don't sit on their hands; they shine. Disciples don't turn people away from following Jesus; they naturally invite others to join the party by virtue of the luminous manner in which they live. Pilgrims in progress don't just walk in the light, they reflect it. Jesus followers shimmer.

Questions for Reflection

1. Does grace ever challenge you to be the presence of Christ to others? How do you respond?
2. Are you ready to continue on this pilgrim pathway even if it leads through hardship and disappointment?
3. In what ways does the unmaking of part-time Christianity demonstrate the victory of light over darkness and confidence over fear?
5. What half measures are you considering abandoning that do not fit with following Jesus?

Share your thoughts regarding half measures at
www.part-time-christian.blogspot.com/

Prayer

We are prepared to make a commitment to the light, Jesus, to shine with passion and integrity. We ask that you live in and through us and that everything about the way we walk this pilgrim path will speak eloquently and point to the truth of the gospel. Thank you and Amen.

twelve

Living Large for Jesus

We pray this in order that you may live a life worthy of the Lord and may please him in every way: bearing fruit in every good work, growing in the knowledge of God.—Colossians 1:10, NIV

One drab weekday early morning, far too early, I crawled out of bed, got dressed, and made my way to a venue way the other side of Tampa. I was scheduled to speak to a group of business leaders gathered for a networking breakfast at a second-rate dining annex in the lobby of a third-rate motel.

The event was on the calendar for a brain-numbing 6:45 AM; coffee, chitchat, breakfast, a few reports, and then my talk. The organizers asked me to give a twenty-minute program and then leave some time open for questions at the end. My topic that particular day was "The Power of Your Story."

Shaking the predawn cobwebs from my head, I worked hard to

establish rapport with the bleary-eyed executives. I shared a few amusing family anecdotes (whose family isn't funny once you pry the lid off?), some dramatic personal history, and honest description of one or two key struggles that have helped—or forced—me to develop a deeper insight. And I threw some challenging questions their way.

It's vital that we know our own story well, I advised, illustrating with inspirational moments from interviews with parents and grandparents. I reminded my audience about the sense of connection that generational storytelling can generate, bringing to life great events in history. Then I drew their attention to the critical importance of understanding where we fit—personally—in this the latest chapter of The Greatest Story Ever Told.

I warmed to my subject. Somehow, despite the hour, the setting, and the bad coffee, the dreary dining room began to brighten perceptibly.

When I finished speaking, the first question came from a sixty-something corporate executive. He appeared worn and weighed down. His suit was expensive but a little tight; his shirt was freshly pressed, but his tie was the wrong color. The expression the man wore was acutely quizzical, oversized, etched deep.

"I have to ask you about your presentation," the man said, tracing a finger around the rim of his coffee cup. "I certainly enjoyed it, but more importantly I couldn't help but notice your unusual enthusiasm. It was almost as if you really believe in everything you have to say."

His implication was clear. Either (a) people simply don't or shouldn't say anything with that much enthusiasm that early in the morning, or (b) I couldn't possibly believe all that stuff I was spouting—could I?

I was taken aback because I honestly couldn't imagine talking on a subject that I didn't care about, and so my answer came out with more candor than usual in such an exchange. Maybe it was too early in the morning; maybe I'd had one too many cups of coffee; maybe it was the Spirit.

"Consider the following," I offered. "First of all, I'm not a morning person, yet I got up at five o'clock today, took a hurried shower, dressed somewhat professionally, took care of the dog and a few other details, made my wife coffee, and then I climbed into my car. Next I fought around sixty minutes of miserable rush-hour traffic. I narrowly avoided three accidents, and I listened to several obnoxious morning radio shows before finding something inoffensive I could tolerate.

"I drove all the way through downtown Tampa, missed my exit, was cursed out by several drivers who evidently weren't lost; and despite their helpful encouragement, I still managed to get turned around twice.

"Finally I found this location, and I arrived a good five minutes early, which was—I have to say—quite the achievement."

I wasn't finished. "After I parked my notes and secured a much-needed cup of coffee, I ate a poor apology for a breakfast before excusing myself so I could go over my remarks and prepare my heart and mind to deliver the short speech that you just heard.

"Believe me," I concluded, "and no offense intended because you're obviously a pleasant group of people to be around and I respect your commitment to one another and this community, but there's no way I would willingly put myself through all that aggravation on a Tuesday morning unless I believed passionately in what I intended to share with you."

A loud silence followed, then a cough, and another pause that lasted just a little too long. The questioner followed up.

"Well, then," he said, half laughing to himself and looking around the room, "you must be the first person we've had this year who believes in much of anything at all. I can't remember the last time we had a program when the person behind the microphone appeared to care much one way or the other about the material he or she presented."

What a tragedy, I thought, *what a sad way to communicate.*

Authenticity is the most powerful tool at our disposal when it comes to getting out this important message about "living as if we mean it." I don't receive invitations to speak because I'm eloquent in front of crowds—I get them because I write a newspaper column and have developed a "community voice." People often make the generous leap of assuming that because I'm a writer I can also speak in public. But they usually do ask me to come back. Why? Because the message always comes directly from my heart, and I am genuinely excited about what I believe.

So I pretty much always accept the invitations—it gets me out of the house, and more often than not there's free food involved. But once I show up, I invariably learn so much more from the people than I could ever hope to give them in return. My lesson that particular day was clear: never allow my public witness to become stale or perfunctory.

What causes, businesses, or—God forbid—faith-based initiatives had been held out like limp handshakes in front of this group of fairly influential business and community leaders? They obviously were ready, and very much hungry, for someone to hold out the word of life (Phil. 2:16).

Clear vision for the hard of hearing

"For this people's heart has grown dull,
   and their ears are hard of hearing,
   and they have shut their eyes;
   so that they might not look with their eyes,
   and listen with their ears,

136

and understand with their heart and turn—
　and I would heal them."
But blessed are your eyes, for they see, and your ears, for they
hear. Truly I tell you, many prophets and righteous people
longed to see what you see, but did not see it, and to hear what
you hear, but did not hear it.—Matthew 13:15-17

Moving away from part-time Christian status is not one decision
but a series of decisions, sometimes several times a day. This journey is a cradle-to-grave adventure, an ongoing challenge, and the
process likely didn't begin in one definitive moment. Progress is
driven by movement—forward and circling back—full of amazing
possibility and the promise of reinvention.

People often asked Jesus to explain what was consequential. We
also need to be focused on what is essential, what really makes a
difference. Just a few elemental tools, the right ones for the job—
that is all we really need.

My life has become a kind of scratch pad where powerful things
are jotted down: images of faith, moments of grace, encounters of
love, evidences of hope, revelation in direct proportion to my ability to listen and also my willingness to open my eyes to see. Not just
to see but to have vision; not just to hear but to feel, touch, taste,
and even smell the unrelenting constant of God's insistent truth.

God's purpose is relationship, restoration, reconciliation. But
there can't be any reconciliation without communication and certainly no communication if we can't or won't listen, say we don't
have the time, or refuse to really try.

Two key elements to this journey are perspective and intention.
God has gifted us with the ability to see from inside our heart. So
do we observe through a wide-angle lens or limit our vision to the
endemic cultural myopia? Do we run free or are we restricted by
blinders? Do we search for new stars with purpose at night or do we
glance up without belief in the middle of the day?

Being a full-time Christian is about cultivating open minds and developing receptive hearts. It's also about staying away from presumption, limiting preconception, and learning enough to steer clear of misconception. It's about being on the right wavelength: "those who have ears will hear" and "those with eyes will be able to see."

The people I know who experience miracles are the people who wake up expecting miracles. One Easter, a member of my adult Sunday-school class shared her journal as a resurrection testimonial. The front cover reads, "Miracles I Have Received," and she expects to fill every page. She inscribed the title in bold letters before she ever started to write. My friend is certainly more likely to encounter wonder than those of us who have already decided miracles do not occur or happen only in the lives of other people.

My wife, Rebekah, found her four-leaf clover only because she took the time to look. Likewise, when I worked nights as a security guard in college, I was the only student who saw shooting stars every time I worked. Why? Because while others were watching television, stealing some shut-eye, or reading trash under harsh lights in the guardhouse, I was outside looking up.

Often when I write I share images of peace, calm, joy, family harmony, stunningly beautiful encounters with nature, whispers of grace, and experiences of devotion. Life can be like that. But more typically I find myself running a few minutes late on a hurried afternoon at a red light, behind a massive pickup truck without a functioning muffler, or alongside a dirty 1988 Chevy with three pairs of twelve-inch speakers boosting two hundred and fifty decibels of "The Fat Boys Live!"

It is precisely at moments like this—overdue at school or day care, overstressed that day at work, maxed out on credit, overdrawn at the bank, out of sorts with family—that the reflexes of a practiced and well-exercised faith get the opportunity—and the imperative—

to kick in. People not in the habit of expecting God's presence will not, in all probability, enjoy it at Fifth Avenue and Main on a busy Tuesday afternoon. Christians conditioned to hearing God only through a preacher Sunday mornings are not about to pick out the voice of the Master over obnoxious music at 250 decibels. Even hurting hearts desperate for a little spiritual healing will remain dry all week long if they fail to actively engage their spiritual core any time other than 11:00 AM, once every seven days, at Sunday school or church.

God is much more creative than our comfort level tends to allow—much more in tune with the tempo of our lives and the various places we find ourselves. In fact, those are the points where God seeks us—through most everything that happens, in every incongruent and often confusing aspect of our personal experience.

As Jesus followers, we are called to cultivate a practiced sensitivity to Christ's presence, to unfold the neglect, to deliberately open the eyes of our souls, and to spend time expectantly in God's Word. The heartbeat of our commitment is to keep Jesus always on our minds.

This "unmaking" of a part-time faith calls us to recognize Jesus as our friend, not a visitor; the embracing of Christ as intimate family, not formal company. Our relationship with Christ is natural with no need for pretense or façade. God is with God's children: not in thunder or earthquake or lightening or fire but simply in the still small voice of a venerable and trusted friend—familiar, credible, and real.

Reversal

Sometimes God effectively turns everything around. To tell the truth, God pulls that move all the time. Turning stuff around is God's modus operandi. It's when we remember to follow Jesus, and when we have the courage to hold fast to the word of life (Phil. 2:16), that God's power is most evident. That's when the prayer "Use me Lord, use even me" has to be the beginning and the end of our intention, because the Spirit will move where the Spirit chooses to move. Beyond that, sometimes the rest of us just seem to be along for the ride.

In an earlier chapter we talked about the idea that—at times—the "membrane" separating the natural world and the spiritual plane is stretched to a point of transparency, creating a time and a place where the two realities overlap more readily. For me, recently, the membrane has been stretched thin. I noticed a kind of shift one evening in the park when three separate groups of people stopped to thank me for honoring God in my newspaper work—the air was simply tingling with the Spirit. The experience continued the next morning at the auto repair shop, where a "chance" encounter with a disillusioned lawyer led to a long conversation about faith.

Later, on my way home, I stopped at the store. At the checkout, the woman ahead turned to speak to the cashier, stopped suddenly, and asked, "Aren't you that Derek Maul who writes in the newspaper?" Two sentences later, right there in the grocery store checkout line, I had the opportunity to minister to someone who needed to understand the power and presence of God in that particular moment. The conversation was brief, but God gave me exactly the right words of hope, of encouragement, and of assurance.

The cashier stood by with her mouth hanging open while the woman, tears streaming down her face, hugged me. "I know it was no accident I came to the store this afternoon," she said. "Thank you for being here."

That night, after dinner, I shared the events of the day with my wife. "Rebekah, it's a tremendous feeling to be used by God just once," I told her, "but I have to admit the last twenty-four hours have been kind of exhausting."

"Welcome to my world," she started to say, but our conversation was interrupted by the sound of the telephone. "Probably a sales call or some politician," I said, "but I'll take a look."

The incoming signal originated from an area code I didn't recognize, but I felt the Spirit urge me to take the call. "Hello," the voice inquired, "is this Mr. Derek Maul?"

"Yes," I said. "Can I help you?"

"Are you the Derek Maul who writes for *Guideposts* magazine?"

"I haven't placed an article in *Guideposts* for several years," I said, curious.

"Well, this one's from 2003," he said, and described the story.

Why on earth would someone track me down and call from the other side of the United States to talk about a short article published sometime in the way-back-when? The magazines in my doctor's office aren't even that old.

"I remember the story," I said. "How did you run across it after all this time?"

"I picked up the magazine in a thrift store," he said. "I read your article, and I couldn't put it down. I'd pretty much lost my faith, and your story has helped me to find my way back to God. I'm having the page framed. It's going up on my living room wall where I can always see it. I called because I wondered if you would please sign it for me if I mail it to your house. And would you please pray for me?"

When we finished our conversation, I hung up the phone, dazed, and went back to the living room to tell Rebekah. "I'm asking God for twenty-four hours off," I said. "I'm not sure that I could take another day like this tomorrow."

Like I said, the membrane has been stretched thin, and I really didn't experience much let-up for a while. To tell the truth, I wonder if the real place such an obstruction is located—the barrier that effects distance and silence between me and God—happens to be around my heart rather than somewhere in the heavens: my spirit neatly cordoned off; God's challenging intervention at a safe distance; my pilgrim progress on hold.

But still, pushing to the surface like insistent growth on a hopeful spring morning, my promise to follow Jesus finds its way, often one tentative footfall at a time. But it's progress all the same and I know where I'm going; finding my way full circle; onward back to the garden.

For me, this is a path of undoing—a journey into unmaking, the unmaking of a part-time Christian. My road has never lent itself to neat bullet points, tidy conclusions, or a series of sequential slides in a PowerPoint. This is a movement away from compartmentalized faith and into fully engaged, transformational, moment-by-moment, live-as-if-I-mean-it Christ-life.

Following Jesus is not for those who seek to be undisturbed; yet I know real peace. Discipleship is more about questions than easy answers, but still I know complete assurance. This unmaking of part-time Christianity is guaranteed to grate against this culture; regardless, I know Jesus. And I know every day and without a shadow of a doubt that I am finding my way home.

> Do not let your hearts be troubled. Believe in God, believe also in me. In my Father's house there are many dwelling places. If it were not so, would I have told you that I go to prepare a place for you? And if I go and prepare a place for you, I will come again and will take you to myself, so that where I am, there you may be also. And you know the way to the place where I am going.—John 14:1-4

Questions for Reflection

1. Do you consider yourself a part-time Christian? Reflect on your progress. Describe the steps you are taking toward full-time status.

2. This is just a short volume. How do you imagine your story might fill in the next illustration, the next chapter, the next installment of the adventure?

3. Ask God right now, in this moment, where the journey will be leading you next? Write down what you think God is saying.

4. How can we let go of our own agendas and invite the Spirit to be our guide?

What comes next in the journey?
Share your insights, thoughts, and questions and
be part of the ongoing dialog at
www.part-time-christian.blogspot.com/

Prayer

We are all pilgrims, Creator God, humble in determined progress. Bless us with your presence along the way; bless us with the guidance of the Holy Spirit; bless us with the companionship of Jesus; bless this world through the ministry of our obedient lives. In your powerful name we pray. Amen.

About the Author

DEREK MAUL, blogger and newspaper columnist, is author of two other books, *Get Real: A Spiritual Journey for Men* and *In My Heart I Carry a Star: Stories for Advent.*

Derek writes in his blogspot profile: "Life is good. It's about living in partnership with my wife, Rebekah, about serving God in the context of our church home, about being the parent of two amazing children, and of both honing and using my particular gifts in order to make this world a better place." Find out more about him at http://derekmaulsblogspot.blogspot.com